The Spirit
of the Apocalypse

WHAT IS THE SPIRIT SAYING TO THE CHURCHES?

William Riley

DOMINICAN PUBLICATIONS
TWENTY-THIRD PUBLICATIONS

First published (1997) by
Dominican Publications
42 Parnell Square
Dublin 1

and

Twenty-Third Publications
P.O. Box 180, 185 Willow Street
Mystic CT 06355

ISBN 1-871552-59-1 (Dominican Publications)
ISBN 0-89622-720-0 (Twenty-Third Publications)

British Library Cataloguing in Publications Data.
A catalogue record for this book is available
from the British Library.

Copyright © (1997) Estate of William Riley

All rights reserved.

No part of this publication may be reproduced, stored in
a retrieval system or transmitted by any means,
electronic or mechanical, including photocopying,
without permission in writing from the publisher.

Printed in the United States of America

Contents

Preface *Carmel McCarthy* RSM	5
Introduction (Revelation 1:1-11)	9
1. Seeing Jesus (Revelation 1:12-20)	19
2. Churches Need Ears (Revelation 2:1 – 3:22)	30
3. The Throne Room of the King (Revelation 4:1 – 5:14)	45
4. Disturbing Sounds of Breaking Seals and Blaring Trumpets (Revelation 6:1 – 9:21)	60
5. Three and a Half Years (Revelation 10:1 – 11:18)	77
6. The Great Sign (Revelation 11:19 – 12:18)	90
7. Unmasking the Pretenders (Revelation 13:1 – 17:18)	108
8. Some Final Scenes (Revelation 18:1 – 20:15)	127
9. The Grand Finale (Revelation 21:1 – 22:21)	144
10. It Is Done! (Revelation 21:1 – 22:21) *Shán Ó Cuív*	145
William Riley (1949-1995) *Carmel McCarthy* RSM	155
William Riley: a Bibliography of Works in Scripture Studies	158
Contributors	160

Preface

This book was written in less than six weeks. Books do not usually get written in such a short space of time. But when it is remembered that these same six weeks coincided with the last six weeks of the author's life, it becomes an achievement of a very different kind. All the more so, since the uninformed reader would never suspect from its contents just how ill and close to death its author knew himself to be.

From a technical point of view, William Riley did not actually finish this book completely, but he almost did. His last sentence occurs early on in what was to have been the final chapter, aptly titled: 'The Grand Finale'. He had only just begun this last chapter two days before being admitted to hospital where, having slipped into a coma, he died four days later.

The last words he entered into the computer shortly before the end contained the dedication he wanted inserted at the beginning of the work: 'To Shán, Caitríona, Carmel, Ann and Theo'. It will become clear to the reader of the final chapter who Shán is. Caitríona Ní Chuív, Shán sister, was a close friend of Bill, and in the last months of his illness her gentle presence and support were an invaluable source of strength to him. The friendship he enjoyed with Ann and Theo Payne stretches back to the early days before their marriage in 1983, and expressed itself in many ways, not least through the skilful line drawings Theo created for two of Bill's most successful books. Finally, my own association and friendship with Bill originated in Carysfort College of Education where we were colleagues in Scripture for many years.

Although unable to complete the final chapter, Bill finished this book in a more radical and prophetic way through the surrender of his life, as he courageously accepted all the pain and helplessness of the four short months between his initial cancer diagnosis and his early death. Before he died he asked his friend, Shán Ó Cuív, to finish that final chapter for him. This Shán has done with great sensitivity to the task enjoined on him, wonderfully integrating into a final synthesis the book's main themes and message.

This *Spiritual Adventure of the Apocalypse* captures all the freshness and enthusiasm that Bill brought to anything he undertook. It reflects a careful and finely-tuned scholarship which permeated all his teaching and research. It also combines his unique ability to communicate the riches of Scripture to any audience with an indomitable sense of humour that remained with him to the end.

Recovering from surgery at the beginning of his final illness, Bill informed us he was going to write a book. Apart from Shán, who knew him better than most, the rest of us listened in disbelief, as we inwardly assumed that this would be impossible, given the advanced nature of his illness. But as the final weeks unfolded we were to learn how unfounded our assumption had been. It was an inspiration to see this book grow, chapter by chapter, as its author faced each day, accepting with courage and in faith the limitations his illness imposed on him. He found nourishment and strength in writing, and a vision which in turn became life-giving for those accompanying him in the last weeks.

It may be of help to readers to note two technical details to which Bill gave special attention in the composition of this book. First, in order to distinguish between the New Testament's overall vision of Church as a spiritual and theological reality, and the individual churches to which John the Seer's work is addressed, he used a capital letter for the former and a lower case 'c' for the latter. Thus the word 'Church' encompasses the People of God in its totality down through the ages, and is synonymous with those rich images the Seer used to symbolise the Church's unity and deeper mystery in Christ (the Woman Clothed with the Sun, the Bride). By contrast, 'church' refers to particular manifestations of the Church (individual churches in first century Asia Minor, as well as the church that constitutes one's local parish, diocese or denominational entity today).

The second detail has to do with using a capital letter for the Temple in Jerusalem. Worship and liturgy form an intrinsic backdrop to the Book of Revelation. John the Seer's roots are thoroughly Jewish; and so, many images in Revelation are drawn from his fond memories of joining in the worship of the Jerusalem Temple. This accounts for the particular way the Seer has linked and interwoven earthly liturgy with what is continuously taking place in all the splendour and eternity of the heavenly Sanctuary.

Readers will also notice that Bill used the words 'Apocalypse' and 'Revelation' interchangeably as titles for the book recording the teaching and visions of John the Seer. The spiritual riches of the Apocalypse take on new meaning when read against the background of reflections penned by one who was soon to participate in its heavenly worship. May the spiritual adventure of this book help its readers enter into the challenges of John the Seer, so that they may genuinely hear what the Spirit *is* saying to the churches today. May this book help deepen the bond between those who have already entered into the glory celebrated in the Apocalypse and us pilgrims still on the journey.

Carmel McCarthy RSM

Introduction

Revelation 1:1-11

I love the Book of Revelation. There are, of course, plenty of people who love the Book of Revelation. There are those whose major weekend pursuit consists of trying to identify which major modern figure is shown by the Apocalypse *really* to be the Antichrist (if only you knew how to look). There are those who use pencil and paper, pocket calculators and spreadsheet software to figure out from Revelation's numbers the exact time for the end of the world (oddly enough, the answer is usually sometime in the next few years). And then there are those who seem to enjoy what comes across as doom and gloom in the book's story. I suspect that they also take more interest in reports of catastrophes and disasters than in any other part of the daily news report.

But there are others, and I like to think that I am to be counted among them. Many artists, for example, have found powerful inspiration in Revelation's word-pictures for works of great visual intensity and beauty. Musicians like Handel have found glittering gems of poetry in Revelation that they have tried to give fitting settings with the silver and gold of their compositions. New Testament scholars have dedicated their life's work to exploring the artistry and theology of the book and have produced invaluable studies that help the rest of us to understand the Apocalypse's message. And then there is the largest group of all, those countless Christians who hear in the book a message of celebration, challenge and – above all – hope. It is in this last group that I feel that I fit best.

Introducing This Book

I am not trying to write a book that will answer all the questions you ever had about the Apocalypse (although, with a bit of luck, it might answer a few). There are other biblical scholars who specialise in the study of Revelation and I'll leave that sort of writing to them. For the past twenty years or more, I have found great spiritual nourishment in Revelation. As the Catholic liturgy presented the book to the Church annually at Easter time, I found its reading a true springtime of the soul. Apart from those works that I have used in teaching New Testament Greek to students, there is no part of the Greek Testament that I have read so frequently or constantly in the original language – not as a study, but as a nourishing spiritual exercise.

And that is exactly what I intend this book to be: a spiritual exercise that may be of use to others. After all, spiritual exercises like spiritual gifts aren't meant for the individual, but for the good of the whole Body. False spirituality is self-centred, but Christian spirituality brushes against others as it reaches out to God. Just because I am doing a spiritual exercise in public doesn't mean that I imagine myself to be some type of expert in the field; it's simply that I'm not ashamed to be seen doing my callisthenics clumsily with the other beginners!

Please forgive this book for being uneven. I will not treat each part of Revelation with equal care, nor work my way methodically through each passage. I will try to draw upon what scholarly knowledge I do possess of the Apocalypse, but I will steer clear of the scholarly debates and differences of opinion (and scholars *are* an argumentative lot). I will occasionally use footnotes to explain technical terms or to give short explanations of background matters. Sometimes passing references will be made to the text of Revelation (and sometimes to other Scriptures) by chapter and verse, but don't feel obliged to stop and look these up as you come across them. These are there to help those who want to see for themselves how the text supports the point I am making. Take what follows as a personal mixture of attention to the biblical text, reflection upon its message for us as a church today and the fruit of prayer – with all the limitations and (I hope) a few of the strengths that such a mixture entails.

The question arises about how this book should be used. About all I can suggest is that it is used best while reading Revelation. Under the title of each chapter, a reference will be made to a part of Revelation (which may be very short or very long). Ideally, this passage should be looked at first (without expecting to understand everything in it), or at least – if you are somewhat familiar with Revelation – be given a quick overview as a reminder of what's in

Introduction *(Rev 1:1-11)* 11

the passage. After the chapter of this book is read, then the text of Revelation can be read again as the basis of your own study, reflection and prayer.

You may have noticed that I have given a passage for this introduction. The passage is Revelation 1:1-11 and will serve as a beginning exercise, but we will use it more for introducing John's Apocalypse rather than looking much at its spiritual content. When we come to use any part of the Scriptures, we gain much more if we know a little bit about the background, what type of writing it is and how the author was trying to communicate his message. In fact, the author of Revelation used these beginning verses to cover some of that territory in his own day, so this is an ideal opportunity to get some background considerations out of the way. If parts of the next two sections are too technical for your taste, feel free to skim through them and skip on to the section 'Good and Evil in the Book of Revelation'. You can always return to the background material if you feel the need.

John the Seer

People have naturally been curious about exactly who was who in the New Testament. Sometimes entirely different people in the life of Christ got mixed together into a single figure in popular religion. The most famous example of that is Mary Magdalene who appears in the gospels as an important witness to the cross and resurrection of Jesus. However, about five hundred years later, some Christians started identifying her with the sinful woman who washed the feet of Jesus with her tears – and Mary's reputation never recovered! That sort of thing makes scholars very nervous about identifying New Testament authors with well-known figures.

There is an ancient tradition that the Apocalypse was written by the apostle John, and it could be right (although few scholars would entertain it today). But it was not the only answer given to the question in early Christianity. Some ancient writers noted that there was a prominent leader in the early Church known as John the Elder, who was not an apostle, and attributed Revelation to him. There seems to have been a suggestion, around the fourth century, that the Apocalypse was written by John Mark, but it never became widely accepted. Many of the ancient writers commented that the

Apocalypse seems to have been written by a someone other than the author of John's Gospel. All the author himself tells us is that his name is John, and the name was nearly as common in his day as in our own. To distinguish him from all the other possible Johns of the early Church, he is sometimes referred to as 'John the Seer'. Even though he doesn't give us much autobiographical information in the book, what he has written tells us much about him.

The most important thing to notice is that John was a Jewish Christian. Sometimes modern Christians forget their Jewish roots and presume that, for a Jew, becoming a follower of Jesus in the first century involved changing your religion. But that isn't the picture that comes across from the New Testament. For an Israelite to become a disciple of Christ meant finding the fullness of everything that had been believed and hoped for in the faith of Israel. Just because converts from outside the Jewish race were not required to keep all the details of the Law didn't mean that Jewish Christians stopped following the practices that had formed and nurtured their faith. The apostles still went to the Temple to pray, and Jewish Christians made their pilgrimages to Jerusalem for the ancient festivals. They followed the Law in the spirit of freedom taught by Christ and there was no contradiction for them in being both Jewish and Christian. The New Testament testifies that St Paul still considered himself to be a member of the Pharisees after his conversion; Paul even implies that his Christian faith is largely the logical consequence of his Pharisaic belief in the resurrection of the dead.[1]

John the Seer was a very learned Jewish Christian, even if he might not have been culturally sophisticated or genteel. Even in translation, John's imagery and expression can strike the reader as rough and raw. His Greek comes across as halting and unpolished (and quite different to the Greek of the Fourth Gospel). But John is

---

1. Acts 23:6-7. Paul's statement may puzzle modern readers who only know Pharisee as a synonym for hypocrisy. The Pharisees were a school of interpretation of the Law in first century Judaism and many, like Paul's teacher Gamaliel, were saintly and are honoured in the New Testament. In the gospels, the Pharisees appear as a stereotype that the readers of the first century would have recognised; the criticisms of them in the gospels are generally aimed at any person (Jewish or Christian) who cares more about human opinion than God's or who gets caught up in 'religion' while neglecting the central law of love.

Introduction (Rev 1:1-11) 13

a poet and artist for all that. He knows the Scriptures of Israel thoroughly and uses them deftly; at times he can conjure up thoughts of whole biblical passages with the use of one or two words. He knew the beautiful ceremonies of the Temple in Jerusalem intimately and knew how to communicate his memories of their celebration. Even though the Jerusalem Temple had been tragically destroyed in 70 AD, we can still catch reflections of the splendour of its liturgies from the pages of the Apocalypse. John and his original audience must have loved being part of those festivities, for he used the recollection of them to whet the appetite for the joys of God's promised future. Yes, knowing that John was a Jewish Christian is very important for understanding his work.

The most striking thing that John tells us about himself is that he received a revelation that he must communicate. He is confined to the island of Patmos, seemingly a prisoner or exile for the faith,[2] and his message is for seven churches on the mainland of Asia Minor (where Turkey is today). We must not imagine that John simply recorded his revelation as he received it like a sports commentator describing a football game in progress. Like others who have felt they received a revelation in later ages (Julian of Norwich and St Catherine of Siena are examples that come quickly to mind), the Seer carefully chose the form and words that he thought would let others know the message. He used images familiar to his readers and put forward symbols that had several layers of meaning. He chose terms and phrases that would make people think of familiar passages from the Scriptures. He did everything he could to unfold the secret revelation that he saw on the Lord's day at Patmos.

Revelation as Apocalyptic Literature

The appreciation of any piece of writing requires a knowledge of what type of writing it is. Normally this doesn't cost us a thought.

2. John mentions that he is on this small volcanic island off the western coast of Asia Minor 'because of the Word of God and the witness of Jesus', but he doesn't really explain the connection. Most read John's comment as referring to some persecution for the faith, perhaps being banished to Patmos in exile (banishment was a frequent punishment in the Roman world). A few suggest that John was there to preach and teach, others that he could have gone there to reflect and pray. The strongest argument is still for banishment but, whichever was the case, John makes it clear that times were difficult for him as a Christian and that, in some way, he was suffering for the faith.

We approach the reading of lyric poetry, comic verse, science fiction, and autobiography all in different ways. Even when reading the Bible, we can see the differences between the legal language of parts of the Law and the poetry of the Psalms, between the humour of Jonah and the solemnity of the Passion accounts, between the grandeur of Job and the simplicity of Ruth.

When we open the Apocalypse, we find a book that differs from every other book of the New Testament. Some of the types of writing in it are familiar from elsewhere: letters, sayings of Christ, hymns of praise; yet even these familiar forms are different. The letters are dictated by Christ in a vision, his sayings are heard from heaven rather than in Palestine and the hymns of praise are sung by celestial choirs.

Revelation fits best into a category of writing referred to as apocalyptic literature. This was a type of religious writing that was used especially from the second century BC to the second century AD when times were dangerous and the prospects for believers – Jews and Christians – looked grim. Apocalyptic literature took situations of great trial for people of faith and tried to show how events made sense in the grand plan of God; the dark curtain of current affairs was lifted by such writers to allow the bright splendour of God's providence to shine through. Apocalyptic could often graphically expose the power of evil at work in the world, but only so that the stronger presence of God might be seen. Recollections of God's promises, accounts of visions, use of mind-challenging symbolism and a pained concern with where the plan of God was leading are all qualities that the Apocalypse shares with many other such writings.

A special word might be in order about the way that apocalyptic literature (including the Book of Revelation) talked about future events. Apocalyptic writers were concerned about the future, but only the ultimate future – that is, the total fulfilment of the divine plan for God's people. At times such authors could use language about the future in much the same way as science fiction writers use futuristic inventions and scientific terms to build an atmosphere and set a scene. Readers who take the details of Revelation (or Daniel or any other apocalyptic writing) as firm predictions of specific future events in human history are simply abusing the text

Introduction (Rev 1:1-11)   15

and ignoring the author's clear indicators that he is expressing himself through symbolic language. John had no interest in writing journalistic accounts of the future; he wanted only to portray the general sweep of God's unfolding plan of struggle, challenge, protection and assurance for those who live by the faith they received through Jesus.

Like many apocalyptic authors, John intended his book to be received in at least two ways. When John writes 'Blessed be the one who reads aloud and those who hear the words of this prophecy', we should immediately realise that this book was written to be read aloud to the Christian communities to which it was addressed. They would hear the story unfold bit by bit, sense the beauty and horror of the images and sense the insistence of the book's rhythms. As they listened to the whole thing from start to finish, they would undoubtedly feel the impact of a message that was for their community by name, wherever they heard it – from Ephesus to Laodicea.

But, at a different level, John also calls for people to puzzle out his meaning and to explore his symbols. His use of Scripture, for example, presumes that some people will know the passages that he refers to. At times, the Seer drops allusions to the Scriptures as if he is marking a trail for the attentive reader to follow into the heart of the faith of Israel, now fully realised in the faith of disciples. Similarly, the way numbers appear in Revelation reflects some of the esoteric thinking and symbolic use that surrounded numbers in much of the ancient world. John's symbols and images are often fashioned from many different sources – pagan, Christian and Israelite – and themselves seem to have a number of levels of meaning. And John calls our attention to these things. He tells us that this particular number requires us to think about it until we understand it, or this detail of another symbol can have at least two references when you look at it through first century eyes.[3]

So we are doing what John intended us to do if we simply listen to the Apocalypse and let the impact of John's work make its mark upon our own faith, as might happen when we hear it read in the liturgy. But if we also sit and ponder it, puzzling it out and tracing its message, we are also doing something that John wanted his

3. See Revelation 13:18 and 17:9-12.

audience to do – as long as we are straining to hear the Word of God through the Seer and not just playing esoteric games or trying to force John's vision to fit some current event in world history. John would have been most disappointed should someone fully interpret this complex book with the head and still let the heart be unmoved.

Besides that, the Seer has guaranteed through the richness of his work that no one, not even the most learned New Testament scholar, will ever be able to claim that every allusion has been fully traced or every symbol completely explored! It doesn't matter if the reader is an expert on the Apocalypse or simply a devout listener to the Word, there will always be the unanswered question, always the opportunity to discover something new to savour, always some fresh fare offered us for the nourishment of our faith.

Good and Evil in the Book of Revelation
Apocalyptic literature is hard for modern readers to appreciate not only because of its unusual way of communicating, but also at times because of the way it looks at the world.

In the modern world, we have a keen sense of human autonomy – that we are responsible for our own decisions and actions – and a sensitivity to how there are many sides to every argument. Perhaps this is why so many modern Western Christians find it difficult to believe in the existence of Satan. Firstly, we recoil at the notion that a person, even a purely spiritual one, could be described as totally evil. Secondly, the affairs of the world seem to be so completely under human control that there is neither need nor place for the interference of a supernatural malicious force to explain them. We feel far more comfortable speaking of the bad things in the world as something that is the normal result of human decision and the laws of nature. We are even hesitant in condemning certain ways of acting; we want to find the nuances, hear all sides of the story, avoid a black and white analysis.

While there are strengths in this way of thinking, it certainly wasn't that of the Seer (or any other New Testament figure for that matter). John was anxious to show that evil was real, powerful and very active in the world in which his hearers were living. More than that, evil had to be seen in superhuman dimensions and confronted in a superhuman way. Still, Revelation presents us with a clear

Introduction (Rev 1:1-11)

picture of [...]   In fact, John's black and
white [...]   deeper sense of human
freedom [...]   believed that people could
make cl[...]   or for the forces of evil.

In Re[...]   introduction, evil casts
only the [...]   in the Seer's reference
to his sha[...]   s, the effect of the war
that evil i[...]   ...... John's book will talk
about. Bu[...] same phrase John also tells us that he shares in 'the Kingdom', and that is really what is at the heart of John's book. The Seer is not neurotically preoccupied with evil, but intensely focused upon God and the Kingdom. If he portrays evil with such force, it is only as a help to his audience to perceive more clearly the reality of God.

Like any theologian, John has his own way of speaking of God. Christians are becoming more and more sensitive today to the wide variety of images of God that are available in the Scriptures and in the world around us; and theologians of every age rightly warn us against thinking that one or other image of God enables us to capture the Infinite One with our tiny little minds. Still, we all have our favourite ways of thinking about God, praying to God and talking about God. To some the very word 'God' primarily conjures up images of power and majesty, to others feelings of intimacy and warmth – and Scripture gives us grounds for both.

For John the Seer, <u>God is awesome</u>. God speaks once in the passage we are considering and those words in 1:8 summarise John's basic picture: ' "I myself am the Alpha and the Omega," says the Lord God, "the One Who Is, and the One Who Was and the One Who Is To Come, the All-Powerful." ' Like most New Testament authors, John uses the title 'Father' for God, but with a difference: in the Apocalypse, God is only referred to as the Father of Jesus, never as Father of believers or of all humanity.[4] The Apocalypse

---

4. While Jesus and the New Testament writers frequently refer to God as Father of believers, there are only one or two references to God's fatherhood of all humanity (Acts 17:28-29 and perhaps Ephesians 4:6). The New Testament uses the image of fatherhood to speak of the special intimate relation between God and Jesus that becomes the privileged relationship of disciples. The image has suffered through unfortunate models of fatherhood, and naturally shifts with evolving models of family life. The New Testament use of the image must always be perceived as warm, caring and protective as well as embodying notions of wisdom and governance.

was written more to express the cosmic sovereign majesty of God rather than God's intimacy with individual believers. This way of picturing God, one that we also find in the words of Jesus, springs naturally from the Seer's Jewish heritage. It was in no way meant to lessen, even less to contradict, the essential picture of God as loving, forgiving and concerned with each person. As a character in the great drama of Revelation, God is often the One unseen and unheard while still remaining the source and goal of all things. God is very much at work in the book, but what we usually see in action are God's agents rather than God.

Yet John makes sure that we realise God is behind all the triumphs and promises that the Apocalypse reveals. St Paul's assurance in Romans 8:28, 'We know that God is working all things together into what is good for those who love him', summarises much of the narrative picture that the Seer unfolds for his audience. The power of God as a power of determined love becomes very important in this context; if evil is real and powerful in John's world view – and it is – then it is essential to note that there is a greater power that is even more real for those who cling to God.

One final point of introduction – John's greeting, 'favour and peace' (1:4), might have escaped us in a casual reading of this passage since we are so used to similar greetings in other New Testament letters. That would be unfortunate, for this phrase beautifully expresses exactly what the Seer is hoping his work will bring, an experience of the favour and peace that can only come from God, Jesus Christ and the sevenfold Spirit.[5] Such should still be our experience of the Apocalypse. Even though it refuses to view the world through rose-coloured cataracts, Revelation begins and ends with the promise and assurance of God and still offers favour and peace to anyone who is willing to receive the Seer's message.

---

5. Readers might note that John has two ways of speaking of the Holy Spirit. He uses the singular 'Spirit' as we do most of the time, but occasionally speaks of 'the seven spirits' as an expression of the fullness and all-pervasiveness of the Holy Spirit. John seems to have had a highly developed and explicit trinitarian theology for such an early stage in Christian thought.

1

Seeing Jesus

Revelation 1:12–20

Most of the portrayals of Jesus you see in traditional stained glass are instantly recognisable as such. The circumstances in which he is shown can be radically different – anything from an Anglican window of Jesus blessing the children to a Catholic window of an apparition of the Sacred Heart – but surprising common agreements cross the denominational and devotional boundaries. If we were to try to build a photo-kit picture from our memories of such windows, it would probably include the following: neither fat nor overly thin, neatly bearded with flowing locks, nothing that could be thought of as rugged in the features, usually dressed in a white garment with an outer garment of either brown or red with sandals and bare head, sometimes displaying emotions such as deep compassion or anguish but usually emotionless. If the figure in the stained glass is smiling, chances are that it's not Jesus.

There is one true story that shows how important even these traditions can be to people. Some place in America in the 1950s, the face of Jesus in a prison chapel's stained glass was smashed deliberately. Despite the horrible things that some inmates had done to merit their sentences, this action seemed to reach a new low and to be beneath any of the prisoners. To everyone's shock, the culprit turned out to be one of the devout Christians of the prison population, and he had a reason for his action: the artists who had fashioned the window had made Jesus look Jewish! Pictures of Jesus, especially in the mind, can be ridiculously mistaken.

Picturing Jesus of Nazareth

Quite apart from how we imagine his physical appearance, we all have our own pictures of what Jesus of Nazareth was like during his earthly life. I have been stunned many times by people who solemnly assure me that Jesus never laughed or smiled; they had received and believed this tradition as if it were a defined dogma of the faith. Their model is the Man of Sorrows, which is a fine biblical model as long as it is kept within its bounds of the Passion and not allowed unduly to affect the reading of everything from the infancy onwards. Scholars at the end of the nineteenth and beginning of the twentieth centuries made an equally silly picture. Since most of them were liberal thinkers of their day, they pictured Jesus as a liberal in their own terms. Their mistake filtered down into the popular pictures as well. I remember, for instance, a friend saying that he could never imagine Jesus forbidding divorce (only the nasty Church authorities could do something so unreal and unfeeling) until I showed him several gospel passages in which Jesus did exactly that.

Going back to that question of Jesus' appearance, two traditional theories about his physical being illustrate the very different directions in which believers can speculate. One tradition, familiar to many Western Catholics, is that, since he was the perfect human being, his physical being must also have been perfect: beautiful, noble, well-formed, not too tall, not too short – and having any other perfection that you could think of. The other tradition was to be found among writers in the early Church, and was based on the statement in Isaiah that there was no beauty or comeliness in the promised Servant of Yahweh. According to this view, Jesus was ugly and disfigured; one version even held that he walked with a limp because one leg was shorter than the other.

Fortunately, the gospels don't bother themselves with such unimportant matters as the length of Jesus' legs or the style of his hair. Yet they still yield an amazing amount of material about what the earthly Jesus was like. Because the pictures of Jesus that we receive from our upbringing and devotion are so strong, we don't always notice what is there between the lines in the gospels from people's memory of being with Jesus. For myself, having read, studied and taught the gospels for many years, I have come to notice a few things that I wouldn't have expected. For instance, Jesus was certainly unconventional. He also had a great sense of humour that comes across in many of the parables. He even seemed to enjoy having people on at times (using puns with poor Nicodemus and the Samaritan woman that don't really come across in translation). He could be rough with people at times, especially with those closest to him, but of course he was never unloving. He was very warm and his friendships were extremely deep. The two different pictures of

Seeing Jesus (Rev 1:12-20) 21

Jesus' friendship with Martha and Mary in Luke 10:38-42 and John 11 show quite a few of these things. Jesus is rough with Martha – not without humour in the retort of Luke 10:41-42 – and in John 11 Martha and Mary feel free enough to point out to Jesus that their brother would not have died had he been quicker in coming. Being able to complain is an essential mark of close friendship. Then too, modern readers can easily forget that religious teachers like Jesus shouldn't have had friendships with women in the first place according to first century Palestinian standards.

Once, when I was reading Mark's Gospel very closely and reflectively during a retreat, it dawned on me that Mark hints at Jesus' tendency to touch people physically; being tactile myself, this was a pleasant trait to discover.

Then too, I've noticed that there were different sides to Jesus just as there are different sides to anyone. He knew the value of fasting, but enjoyed taking part in sumptuous banquets. He loved the poor, but he could socialise with the rich. Reconciliation was the goal of so much of what he said and did, but he was not afraid of causing division. He could be gentle and patient with one person and make hard demands of someone else. For all his warmth and affection towards people, Jesus needed to be alone quite a bit. He was responsive to people's needs, but not always in the way they would have expected or wanted. Like everyone else, Jesus had to make decisions that others would criticise; in Mark 1:35-39, for instance, we get the impression that Peter thought that Jesus should get back to helping the sick rather than bothering with praying and preaching (and I'm sure that quite a few of the sick would have been on Peter's side). The one thing that no one can escape about Jesus of Nazareth was that the central focus in his life was his relationship to his Father – that drove him to do and say everything he did.

As with everyone else who builds a picture of Jesus of Nazareth, I have a tendency to concentrate on the things that I like and to overlook those aspects that I'm less comfortable with. Because I know I'm doing this, I need constant contact with the gospel text (and not just my favourite parts of it) to keep the whole picture in mind. If my picture of Jesus and his teaching isn't challenging me as well as comforting me, it is a fair indication that I have managed to mould an idol as false as anything that ever had incense burned before it in a pagan temple, and twice as dangerous.

Models of Jesus Today

As if our pictures of Jesus as he lived and walked in Palestine weren't varied enough, people really begin to differ when they think about how Jesus fits into their own world and lives. I have found all of the following ways of thinking among Christians who take their faith seriously. Sometimes the models overlap, sometimes people switch from one to another according to the situation. In giving thumbnail descriptions of the various models, one inevitably tends to ignore the nuances that adherents of these models would make if they were challenged to be theologically more precise. But if we are honest we might find that one or other model comes fairly close to describing our own natural way of thinking about Jesus.

The first model pictures Jesus primarily as a moral teacher and example. A colleague of mine who is a fine religious educator as well as an excellent theologian once pointed out to me that, here in Ireland, this is the most common way that Jesus is presented in the classroom and often from the pulpit. What is most important about Jesus is what he told us to do and the example he gave in his life. This of course says something about the way some people think of religion: religion is more about action than faith. In contemporary society this attitude often translates into making religion more about changing the world than about changing yourself. To take but one example of the moral model of Jesus in action, when people trained in theology or religious studies think this way, they often concentrate on Jesus as a political figure who tackled the injustices of his own society. The variations on this model are numerous. On the one hand, some make very literal interpretations and applications of everything Jesus said that could be taken as a commandment (whether he intended it as such or not). On the other hand, for some people Jesus acts as a vague moral example – I think hazily about the sort of thing that Jesus might have done and then make my moral decision for today.

A different model of Jesus' relationship to the people's lives bases itself on imputing an overriding sternness to his person; we might summarise it as Jesus the Judge. Christ is primarily the One

Seeing Jesus (Rev 1:12-20) 23

who has laid down the law and now watches to ensure that it is kept to the smallest detail. This model has taken over when Christians become terribly straight-laced, even imaging at times that infringing social conventions and etiquette would be as repugnant to Jesus as breaking the commandments. Those who hold this model often feel that Jesus would certainly disapprove of any person or action that they disapprove of, and largely for the same reasons. This stern model is also at work in a different way when individuals begin to worry about unintentional slips and mistakes as if these were deliberately sins against God. An extreme form of this model lurks in the back of the minds of people whose Christianity is rigid and joyless or who have been crippled by scruples. They have forgotten that the basic term for the story and message of Jesus is Good News.

Many people are happiest in using a model that I will call 'Jesus the Bloke'. Such an approach takes the important truth of Jesus' full and utter humanity and brings it down paths it was never meant to go. It tends to take one's own human habits and attitudes – even failings – and to project them straight onto Christ. In one version of this model, Jesus is happy with whatever you're happy with yourself. Whole dimensions of discipleship – such as conversion, challenge and the cross – don't have much of a place in this picture of a Christ who is perfectly content with you just the way you are. This model can also undermine the role of the teaching of Jesus for disciples; if I find myself in disagreement with something Jesus said or did – well, he might have been having a bad day or just giving *his* opinion.

Then, at the other extreme, for some Jesus is simply God. It is not uncommon for people to do something the New Testament never does, to use the word 'God' as if it were Jesus' name.[1] When left unbalanced by an equally strong awareness of the humanity of

---

1. The New Testament uses 'God' as a description or a title for Christ several times (such as John 1:1 and 20:28), but when 'God' is used as a name the word always refers to the First Person of the Trinity. Phrases like 'God was born in a stable' or 'God died on the cross for us' would have sounded very strange to the authors of the New Testament. Although there is nothing wrong with this way of speaking, theologically it is very imprecise. One or other of the classic heresies in Church history might even lurk behind it, such as the one that denied the distinction of the Persons in the Trinity or some of the ones that held that the divinity of Christ is a way more real than his humanity. I will keep to the New Testament usage throughout, and restrict my use of 'God' as a name to references to the First Person of the Trinity.

Christ, this model inevitably distorts the way that people picture Jesus in his earthly life. I have known people who found it very hard to believe that Jesus had to learn to talk, walk or anything else that is part of growing up. Underplaying the humanity of Christ has the sad effect of making Jesus distant and even unsympathetic to the limitations that our own humanity confronts us with. According to this model, Christ is there to be prayed to, placated and adored but not really to be identified with. We can even excuse ourselves from following his teaching and example with the all too familiar phrase, 'Ah, yes, but he was God!'

The number of models Christians have devised is nearly limitless. Models of Christ have been, and continue to be, fashioned from such diverse viewpoints and philosophies as feudalism, Marxism, feminism, triumphalism and romantic sentimentality. Each model can have some truth behind it and every one can easily be turned into a caricature. When the mainstream Christian tradition – Catholic, Orthodox, Anglican and Protestant – speaks of Christ theologically, it demands that we hold at least two models in our heads at once: Christ is fully divine, fully human. Keeping hold of both ideas simultaneously is not an easy task, but making the effort (even knowing that we might make a few slips) is worthwhile. When we think of Jesus as fully human, we can befriend him, confide in him and form a fully human relationship with him. When we remember that he is also fully divine, we are drawn into the loving relationship of obedience, intercession and adoration that he offers us. Thinking about Christ and fashioning models has been and continues to be part of deepening our awareness of Jesus, but getting the balance right hasn't always been easy. Novels and plays can be written in a few weeks, but the simple words about Christ that we proclaim in the Creed took centuries to compose!

A Revelation of Jesus Christ

John the Seer did not make the mistake of having a single one-dimensional model of Christ. Throughout the book, John presents us with a variety of images to show how Christ relates to his followers and to the world. For the author, the entire Apocalypse is 'A revelation of Jesus Christ' (1:1) both of the message and of the person.

Seeing Jesus (Rev 1:12-20)

After he introduces the work, John shows us the first image of Jesus in 1:12-20. I don't think that anyone could capture its details of snow-white hair and fiery eyes in a stained glass window, or that they would even be tempted to try. Like most of John's work, this picture was meant to be received with the ears rather than seen with the eyes or sketched out on paper. Christ as described in these verses is overwhelming and cosmic in his dimensions, his appearance far more wondrous than anything people saw in Cana or Capernaum. The Seer does tell us the impact this new appearance could have: the author fell like a dead body in fear. Yet John also tells us that this response, although understandable, was not the proper one. The awesomeness of Christ was not there to make John frightened; before he could really receive the revelation, the Seer had to put aside his fear.

The words of Christ about himself in 1:17-18 express in their own way the twofold Christian affirmation of his divinity and humanity. In terms that echo the words of his Father in the very first part of the book, Jesus states that he is 'first and last'; but his humanity is also recalled when he identifies himself as the one who was dead but is now alive. As John will gradually show us, the human life of Christ, particularly in his death and rising, is the key event that lies behind the entire Apocalypse and that will determine the whole future of humanity.

 The vision that John receives combines two separate models the author has of Christ and both come to him from his Israelite heritage. Christ is identified as the Son of Man,[2] a term Jesus used for himself and that was developed richly in the New Testament writings. Due to its centrality in early Christian tradition, this model was highly theological for John and his audience. The second model is no less theological, but somewhat more easily pictured: Jesus appears dressed as the great High Priest ministering before God in the heavenly Sanctuary. Between them, these two models highlight two central points around which the Seer will concentrate much of his book.

---

2. The phrase would be better translated as 'Son of Humanity' since the Greek term is inclusive, but even inclusive language translations tend to keep the familiar phrase in its New Testament occurrences.

The Son of Man

The image of Christ as Son of Man in the New Testament owes much to Daniel 7:9-14. Daniel, like the Seer, is recounting strange apocalyptic visions. Just when he sees a vision of the powers of evil gaining total control, Daniel is given a new vision:

> I watched as thrones were put in place and the Ancient of Days sat down. His clothing was snow white and the hair of his head like pure wool. His throne was like flames of fire, its wheels like the blazing fire.

Then another figure appears in Daniel's vision:

> I saw in the visions of the night and – Look! – with the clouds of heaven came one like a Son of Man. He approached the Ancient of Days and was presented before him. To him was given dominion, majesty, kingship and all nations, peoples and languages will serve him. His dominion is an eternal dominion that will not pass, his kingship one that will not perish.

The Seer presents us with a picture of the Son of Man that also implies his divinity, for John has incorporated aspects of the Ancient of Days into the image of the Son of Man. By showing Jesus as Son of Man in this way, John makes a statement that all of his audience would immediately understand: Jesus is the One around whom world history will revolve. The kingship belongs to him now, and John will show how Christ will claim his Kingdom and begin the fullness of his rule. There is a contrast between the way the Seer thinks about the relationship between Christ and history and our own way of speaking. We are used to thinking about Jesus as a great figure of history influencing the past, but John sees him as One who controls the present and the future – and not just as an influence, but as the One in whom all things will either reach their goal or perish.

In the Midst of Lampstands

When the Seer presents Christ to us dressed in a long robe and standing in the midst of seven candlesticks, he means us to think of the high priest in the Sanctuary of the Jerusalem Temple ministering to God on behalf of the people. The Sanctuary now, of course,

Seeing Jesus (Rev 1:12-20)

is heaven itself of which the Jerusalem Temple was meant to be a symbol. The Seer shows us that Jesus has gone beyond the symbols and now is in the reality itself.

[...] the Apocalypse, John wants to draw us into the [...]hip. John wants us to penetrate the Israelite and [...]ical rituals (of which he is very fond) by using the [...] hearts and minds to see what lies beyond them. [...]ot simply one of the trappings of religion for John. [...]d upon the liturgy and its celebrations as containing [...]g potentials. The worship carried out by God's [...]or him the most important expression of God's [...]a participation in its coming. As High Priest, Christ [...] of the great sacrifice and the one who is now leading [...]ion from human history into God's future; those who follow the High Priest with their joyful shouts are being made into a Kingdom for God. For the Seer, worship is not just the icing on the cake of Christianity whose only important ingredients are being nice and doing good; worship is the heart and soul of a religion that interweaves Christian commitment, action and faith with the realities of God's eternal Kingdom.

Looking at the picture of Christ in 1:12-20, we cannot ignore the lampstands that are mentioned at the beginning and end of the vision and that are identified as seven churches of Asia Minor. In this way, John asserts at both start and finish that Jesus is ministering, not only in the heavenly Sanctuary, but also in the midst of the Church. The Church is to be found with Christ and Christ with the Church. The relationship between Christ and the Church has many facets for John and these are brought before his readers at different stages of his book for their viewing and pondering. What is identified as a revelation of Jesus at the beginning of the Apocalypse turns out to be a revelation of the Church as well, as we shall see.

The mention of seven lampstands provides a good opportunity to note that John generally uses his numbers symbolically. As a symbolic number, seven generally stands for completeness and fullness so that, in the Apocalypse, what can seem to be seven different items at first glance is really a sevenfold unity. The seven lampstands give us a good example of this symbolism: for John, the seven lampstands stand for seven very individual and identifiable Christian communities, but they also stand for the unified reality of the whole People of God. Don't imagine that there are other rooms with other lampstands symbolising other local churches in the Seer's picture. This is the only Sanctuary for John, and by numbering the seven churches John intends to tell us that the sevenfold Church of God is present before God there in its entirety.

John's image of the lampstands goes back to the tradition of a sevenfold lamp that was to burn continuously before God's presence in the Sanctuary and of tending this light being a specifically priestly task. In John's choice of lampstands in the Sanctuary as a symbol for the Church, we begin to see here the relationship that exists for the Seer between God, Christ and the Church: the Church is before God and Christ is in its midst. Just as the priests in the Jerusalem Temple were solely responsible for examining and trimming the lampstands there, now the task of ensuring that the Church is burning brightly falls to the great High Priest alone. His total dominion over the Church, as well as his care for it, is represented by the seven stars of the seven churches held in his powerful right hand. The relationship between the risen Jesus and his Church is protective, dynamic and challenging. In the next section of the work, John will reveal to us more of what this relationship means in more concrete terms and what the High Priest's concerns are as he tries to ensure that the churches' lamps stay alight.

The revelation John received began with a vision of Jesus that was as startling to him as it might be to us. It certainly lacks the cosiness and sentimentality that much Christian devotion would prefer. John's vision embraces images of Christ's utter lordship over history, his awesome divinity, his historical humanity, his relationship to his Church. It would not be possible for us to embark with the Seer on his spiritual adventure without this vision before our eyes. This is not the only image of Jesus that will be presented to us in John's book, but it is the one that will help us most to see and appreciate the totality of the vision John is communicating. And if John's overwhelming vision makes us expand our usual models for Jesus, what harm? After all, those who choose to be totally complacent with their personal theologies should be warned against reading the Seer's Apocalypse. It is certainly not a book for those who want to play at fashioning their own idols.

Questions for Reflection and Prayer

1. What images of Jesus are most familiar to you? When was the last time your reading of gospel passages led you to notice something unexpected about Jesus?

2. Which of the 'Models of Jesus' is closest to how you think of Jesus? Are you willing to let gospel texts challenge as well as comfort you?

3. John sees Jesus as one who controls the present and the future – and not just as an influence, but as the one in whom all things will either reach their goal or perish? How does this strike you?

4. Throughout the Apocalypse John the Seer tries to draw his readers into the wonderful mystery of worship, for him the most important expression of God's kingdom and a participation in its coming. What elements of the Seer's vision have relevance for your understanding of worship today?

2
Churches Need Ears

Revelation 2:1 – 3:22

There are few English words that are more capable of conjuring up such a variety of images in different people than the word 'church'. For many ordinary Catholics, to take one example, the word raises immediate thoughts of bishops, nuns and priests. On the other hand, I'm sure that for many Catholic clergy and religious the word implies the authorities in Rome, and I sometimes wonder who fills the mental picture for the authorities in Rome. Staying with Catholic usage, the word can mean a building, a local parish, a diocese or all the Catholics in a nation or rite. And we can use the word to speak of the whole communion of Catholics worldwide, other denominations of Christians or (most properly of all) the entire People of God whose limits and demarcations are measured by God alone.

In many ears, the word 'church' bristles. It carries with it political overtones, questions of power, problems and turmoils. It reopens wounds of some injury done by this or that priest, some mistake made by a religious, some hypocrisy of a person who was more devout than loving. The pages of Church history are filled with stories of sad mistakes, vicious divisions and tragic scandals. The Church's past and present make easy targets. A person doesn't have to be very involved in religion in order to find something to criticise, even to get angry over, once a discussion turns to the Church.

Thinking 'Church'

There is, of course, a different approach to Church and it surfaces throughout the New Testament.[1] According to this view, the Church is intrinsically and intimately united to the mystery of

---

1. The New Testament contains a variety of ways of thinking about the Church, but these have enough in common to fashion a unified collage for our purposes here. If we really want to appreciate what the New Testament has to say about the Church, we would not only have to investigate such authors as Matthew, John and Paul quite separately; we would also have to consider how images and ideas are used with different nuances and how they develop over time – even in the same group of writings.

Christ. That doesn't mean that the New Testament authors were ignoring the divisions, sins and problems that were to be found in the Church even in their day. As we shall see, the Seer seems to be more grieved about such things than many people who give out about the Church today.

But the New Testament writers never lost sight of the fact that, in some way and for all its faults, Christ was to be identified with his Church, that he loves the Church tenderly like a spouse, and that he promised to be with it until the end of time. Where so many of us see a creaky and defective human organisation, the New Testament sees and talks about the Body of Christ, the True Vine, the Spiritual Temple made of living stones to ensure God's presence with humanity. The sharp distinction that we so often assume exists between Christ and the Church is not to be found in the New Testament. For the New Testament and its authors, the promise and presence of the Spirit of Jesus in the Church means that Christ and the Church cannot be separated, in their day or in ours, for the Spirit of Jesus is greater than human failure.

Prolonged exposure to the New Testament writings has coloured my own point of view. For me, the Church is essentially the People of God; it has faces that I can see, hands at work and voices raised in prayer all around me. The Church shines with the faith of such people and is bejewelled with their love. I know that the Church I can see is but the tip of an iceberg that I can barely imagine. It includes people whose culture would be nearly as incomprehensible to me as their language. It is not defined by neat denominational categories and boxes on census forms. It traces back through history, and Abraham and Sarah are as truly members of the Church as I am.

It is a special joy to me that the seeds of faith, hope and love that God planted at the Church's beginning have been flowering and fruiting ever since, that every member of the Church can feast on the harvest. The Church is so intrinsically bound to the mystery of God's Spirit that for me to break in the creed between professing my faith in the Spirit and professing my faith in the Church would be a distortion.

There is also a dark side to my awareness of Church, however. I accept to my pain that those who are prominent in the Church (be it in a local parish or in the worldwide structures) make their mistakes, have their faults, and provide much raw material for scandal and gossip. I freely admit that the Church in its human aspect has been, is now, and always will be, in need of serious reform; and I hunger for the reform to take place. I am amazed that those who view the Church as a purely human reality could want to remain members of it, unless they could see some way to turn membership to their temporal advantage. I know there is much to question and criticise about the Church, but ultimately I ask myself if the dark side is where the focus of my thinking about Church should be – and the answer, that sometimes comes only after a struggle, is always No.

When the negative aspects of the Church threaten to overwhelm me, I take comfort in the fact that the Church belongs to God alone, as does its destiny. Despite its blemishes, the Church will always bear the presence and voice of Christ and remain the chosen dwelling of God in the world. The glimpses of the divine that can be seen in the Church, even at times through a very human fog, make its considerable imperfections bearable, yet still frustrating and at times very painful.

Seven Real Churches

As a spiritual and theological reality, there is only one Church, the whole communion of saints (and only God knows precisely where it begins and ends). However, the more we speak of Church in concrete terms, the more we find ourselves really talking about 'churches': the church that is my parish or diocese, my national church, my denominational church, other denominational churches, or any combination of these working together.

At the beginning of Revelation, the Seer encourages us to think of the Church in these very concrete terms. Throughout his book he restricts his use of the word 'church' to refer to one or other of the seven Christian communities to which his work is addressed. Even though he will show us a very rich and developed picture of the unified Church and God's plan for it, the Seer combines this with an intimate knowledge of his individual churches and concern for them in very concrete circumstances. Yet by using the symbolic number seven, John communicates his sense of the larger unity of which these individual churches are a part.² In this way he keeps the balance. He avoids the temptation of constructing a picture of Church that is either overly spiritualised on the one hand or, on the other, too restricted to an existence in time and space.

The opening vision of Christ gave us a reminder of the spiritual reality of the Church and its unity, but his concentration in the letters of Revelation 2-3 turns very much to the individual churches. Still, John has not written a series of private covering letters to different communities. He makes sure that each church hears what is said to the others. Even though each letter is carefully tailored to a specific church, each one contains things that the others needed to hear. That is clear from the bugle call contained in each of the letters: 'Anyone with ears must listen to what the Spirit is saying to the churches!' Like the churches themselves, the letters are both individual and unified in John's eyes. Their messages must be heard together and heard by all.

The letters of Revelation 2-3 still resound with the Spirit's voice. The Church affirms their relevance for us today by reading them as Scripture. Yet the letters are so intimately tied to the specific circumstances of seven individual first century communities that it is hard to read them or to hear their universal message without making some reference to their particular settings. To that end – and to get a better feel for the world of John and his audience – we will now take an imaginary package pilgrimage to the east coast of Asia Minor: the pilgrimage has been organised for visitors from Rome who are pagans, not Christians, and it leaves at the end of the first century.

> We arrive in Asia Minor and head for the great city of *Ephesus* with its population of nearly a quarter of a million. We will spend a good few days here, not only because we are exhausted from the sea journey, but because there is so much to see. Our

---

2. John's decision to use these seven individual churches to represent the whole Church becomes a little more significant when one remembers that there were far more than seven local churches in the immediate region – and the Seer would have known these churches too. At least one of these unnamed communities, that of Colossae, was far more prominent than some of the ones John actually does address. John has chosen these seven because he has indeed something urgent to say to them as real communities of real people, but the number is kept down to seven so that the symbolic number seven can carry the connotation of a larger unity of Church in his vision.

guide warns us that Ephesus's recent demotion from its status as provincial capital by the Roman authorities is still a sore point, and some of the locals may treat Roman visitors a bit coolly. Most people still consider Ephesus as the main city of the region in financial and cultural terms. Everyone in the group wants to see the Temple of Artemis, one of the seven wonders of the world. It houses the miraculous statue that fell from heaven, and some take extra time to make their special devotions to this popular fertility goddess. Quite a few also want to see the temples of the imperial cult,[3] among which is one of the earliest temples to Julius Caesar in the region. With a theatre that seats 20,000 and its fame as a centre for gladiatorial displays, we find plenty of opportunity for entertainment of every kind.

After we leave Ephesus, we head northwards towards *Smyrna* and more temples, including the earliest temple to the goddess Roma in Asia Minor. The guide tells us that it is a city that technically 'died' hundreds of years before – its inhabitants had been scattered and the city destroyed. But the exiles never let the memory of Smyrna die out and the city was brought to life again by their descendants generations later. The rich variety of shops and goods available in Smyrna makes demands on many pilgrim pockets. A few of the group comment with disapproval that the Jewish population in the city has been allowed to become a little too influential.[4]

---

3. This term 'imperial cult' will keep cropping up in our study of the Apocalypse and a brief explanation is in order here, even though a longer consideration will be given in chapter seven. The word 'cult' in this phrase does not have its usual connotations of some fringe religious grouping that separates itself from society; 'cult' here retains its more technical meaning of a system of worship and belief. The imperial cult was the official state worship throughout the Roman Empire. It centred on the rituals that honoured the goddess Roma (who can be considered a divine personification of the city of Rome) and the emperors. New religions were often devised in the ancient world to help hold peoples together in new political groupings and to give them common allegiance to the state. The Roman imperial cult did this effectively and was particularly popular in the eastern part of the empire.

4. Most first century Romans would have been very anti-Jewish. The religious and cultural differences that Jews insisted on maintaining in their faithfulness to God were taken as an insult by the Romans who could blend different religions together without a thought. In political terms, the Jews would have been seen as rebellious and ungrateful trouble-makers. The Jerusalem Temple was destroyed in 70 AD during a war between Rome and Judea and there would be a further destruction of the city itself in a war of the early second century. Some non-Jews (or Gentiles as they are usually called) did admire the religion of Israel and became worshippers of God, but did not always become full

Two extremely devout members of our pilgrimage group can hardly restrain their excitement as we approach *Pergamum*. They keep talking about the great altar dedicated to Zeus and all the gods that tower over the city and the impressive temple of Roma and Caesar Augustus that we will see. Some of the group (who have filled in our long evenings with numerous and detailed accounts of all their aches and pains) joined the pilgrimage just to get to another shrine, the shrine of the healing god Asclepius, where many world-renowned physicians have worked in their day. Who knows? They might leave a few ailments behind them in exchange for a sacrifice or two to Asclepius and a few denarii for expert medical attention. The guide encourages us not to overlook Pergamum's famous library, but there are so many shrines and such little time.

We begin heading south-eastwards and inland to *Thyatira*, and many in the group wonder why. Even though it is small and provincial, the garrison town of Thyatira can hardly be avoided; it was strategically placed so that armies could be stationed at the crossroad of major routes. Very religious members of the group have to content themselves with prayers at a shrine to Apollo and other minor temples. Some find the local handicrafts interesting, especially the exotic reddish-purple cloth particular to the dyers of Thyatira and the special type of bronze made there.

Continuing in the same direction, we arrive at *Sardis*, still a significant city even though it has known better days. Persians, Greeks and we Romans all once treated it as the leading city of the region, but its centre now bears visible scars of military conquest, earthquake and disuse. Exotic religions are to be found in this city. The earth-goddess Cybele, whose fertility rituals are considered to be over-the-top by most of our group, is worshipped here under the guise of Artemis. Then, too, there is a notable presence of the Jewish religion – some even say that the Jewish nonsense has infected one of the shrines in the city – but we haven't made a sacred pilgrimage to get involved in that sort of thing. One of the pilgrims comments that we should have spent more time in Pergamum and the guide pretends not to hear.

---

converts to Judaism and its demanding life-style; these Gentile followers were referred to as 'God-fearers'.

Things are a bit better at *Philadelphia*. The city is prosperous and its rich athletic, cultural and religious life has earned it the nickname of 'little Athens'. Because of the help that the emperor Tiberius gave it after an earthquake disaster, the city is proud of its devotion to the emperor cult, and we Roman visitors are at last treated with some of the honour befitting citizens of the capital. Once more, we note the strong presence of the Jewish religion, but, sad to say, these things can happen in the best of places.

Our last stop, the inland city of *Laodicea*, is a true wonder. The city prides itself on the fact that when it was devastated by earthquake it could refuse outside help and rebuild itself entirely from its own resources (unlike Philadelphia). The city excels in its devotion to Zeus and to the sun god Apollo, but naturally the imperial cult is not neglected. The Jewish population numbers many thousands and there were legal disputes about their special religious privileges some twenty years ago. Laodicea is famous as a medical and banking centre and there are many amenities, including a stadium, baths, beautiful public buildings and fountains. Once we sample the water, many of us feel that baths and fountains might be the best use for it. The city's water supply comes from hot springs down a long aqueduct. By the time it reaches Laodicea it is lukewarm and some of our group find it a bit nauseating. We might not envy the Laodiceans their water, but we certainly leave envying them their wealth.

John the Seer knew the region well and didn't have to join us on that tour. When he looked at these cities and the churches in them, things appeared very differently through his eyes. The letters hint at the connections John thinks of. Ephesus's loss of its status as capital was nothing compared to the danger of its church's loss of status before God. Smyrna's story of civic death and rebirth pales in comparison to the story of the One who died and is risen. To pagans, Pergamum may be a stronghold of devotion to the state gods, but to John it is the throne of Satan. The little military town of Thyatira that had known so many attacks from without, is now the stage for a spiritual warfare; its Christian inhabitants need encouragement to conquer the evil forces within the community. The church at Sardis, like the city it inhabits, is in decline and

Churches Need Ears (Rev 2:1-3:22) 37

decay. The crowns given at the athletic contests of Philadelphia become a symbol of the crowns that the faithful Christians there are earning in contests with their spiritual opponents. The community of Laodicea may live in a wealthy city, but they have neglected the real wealth that only Christ trades in; their devotion is as lukewarm and as nauseating as their water supply. John not only knows these churches intimately, he shows that he cares about them passionately.

Inspecting the Lampstands

When we first inspect the seven letters ourselves, we might be struck by the common shape they all take. Each begins with a title of Christ related to the opening vision. Each contains a future promise for those who respond to the message. Each states a message tailored to the particular community, as well as a call to all the churches to listen to it.

When we turn our attention to the letters' content, we also find that some concerns keep recurring. It is easy and natural to think about these as the concerns of the author of Revelation (as we have tended to do so far), but that is not the way John saw them. John doesn't put his own name to these letters. They differ from all the other letters in the New Testament because, the Seer tells us, they bear the signature of Christ.

The seven churches were first mentioned in 1:11-12 where John actually shows them to us as part of his initial vision of Jesus. We didn't see them in flesh and blood terms at that stage. We saw their spiritual reality: the churches burn in God's presence as sacred lampstands and Jesus the High Priest stands in their midst. That combination of lampstands and High Priest spills over from the vision into the letters, and it conjures up a powerful image for anyone familiar with the worship of Israel. The seven-branched candlestick (or *menora*) was such a striking piece of furnishing in the Jerusalem Temple that, even now, it acts as a beautiful symbol for the faith of Israel. It was considered to be far more holy than any candlestick in any church today. No volunteer would think of polishing it, no parish worker would have the responsibility for filling up its supply of oil. It was considered to be so sacred that it had to be tended by the priests and by the priests alone.

John has written sections of the Apocalypse as if he were telling us about the celebration of a great festive liturgy in which he had taken part. One memory John would have had of worship in Jerusalem was standing amidst the packed congregation in the Temple courts and catching sight of the high priest in his splendid garments beginning the solemn ceremonies.[5] The first part of the morning liturgy in the Temple, particularly on great feasts, was the priestly inspection of the lamps and – if needs be – their trimming and rekindling. No wonder, then, that Revelation begins with Jesus the High Priest inspecting, trimming and rekindling the seven lamps that should be burning steadily before God. Once again it must be stressed that the Seer tells us that these letters are not coming from him; the words and phrases may be his but, for John, all the thoughts are Christ's. John is only a tool the High Priest is using to get those lamps going.

When we ask what the High Priest is looking for in his inspection of the lampstands, we find we can identify a few items. We keep coming across the term 'works', and we can see that the High Priest expects an active, practical side to discipleship.[6] But we would be mistaken to translate this term as meaning activities and tangible accomplishments. John is not thinking about how many hours the community has clocked up on missionary work, its percentage of growth *per annum*, the success of its fund-raising or the number of its active, well-organised committees. The High Priest is inspecting the attempt, not coldly demanding tallies of results. As we can tell from the warning in 2:23, the place that Christ inspects first and foremost for works is the mind and heart; if things are right there, then whatever flows from there will be something wonderful – no matter how anyone else apart from the High Priest might judge it. On the other hand, what some might see

---

5. Those of us with no experience of worshipping in the Jerusalem Temple can get some sense of the feeling of awe that the high priest could inspire by looking at Sirach 45:6-16 and 50:5-21.

6. The term 'works' is a two-edged word in the New Testament. Paul often uses it as a negative term to describe the foolish efforts some made thinking that they could justify themselves before God by keeping the Law (as in Romans 3:20-21 or Galatians 2:15-16) – as if salvation were something we earned rather than the wonderfully undeserved gift of God. But the term is also used very positively to describe the attempts disciples make to put their faith into action, even when these aren't very successful from a human point of view (see John 3:21, 1 Corinthians 15:58 and James 2:17).

as wonderful accomplishments and triumphs can be judged worthless by the High Priest; that was the very case with the church at Sardis (as 3:1 shows). Our own material models of success have nothing to do with how the High Priest evaluates works; after all, his own great work involved what many saw as the dismal failure of the cross. Letting go our self-imposed demands of success and achievement and taking hold of the High Priest's standards instead would free most of us from a lot of the worry and heartbreak that we imagine we have in the Lord's service.

The inspection reveals that some of the lamps seem to be struggling to keep alight in extremely adverse conditions. The strength of the imperial religion in Pergamum was a force that the local church had to reckon with; one member, Antipas, had already given his life for his faith. Another source of trouble for the churches came from some Jews opposed to Christianity. The fierceness of the rivalry resulted in Jews accusing Christians before the civil authorities; this would bring some disciples real hardship, imprisonment and even the threat of death. The churches had to keep their flames alight despite such attempts to quench them (2:9-10).[7] The High Priest watches the lamps that are fluttering because of such pressures and trims them with encouragement and praise, but always insisting on endurance.

Not all of the flickering is due to outside draughts, however. Some people who called themselves disciples were trying to lead the churches astray, and (it would seem) were having some success. There had been false apostles at work in Ephesus, teachers with a rather liberal attitude to the state religion in Pergamum and a prophetess of like mind in the church of Thyatira. John also refers to a group of 'Nicolaitans' active in two churches. These could

7. Since people today consider Christianity to be a separate religion from Judaism, we find it hard to appreciate that the relationship between Christians and non-Christian Jews was very different at the time John wrote. First century Christianity saw itself primarily as the true expression of the faith of Israel and the real bearer of the promises made to God's People. Outsiders, if they were aware of Christianity at all, would have seen Christians as forming just a branch of Judaism, like the Pharisees or Sadducees, and wouldn't have cared much about the differences. For John and his communities – most of whom would have been Jewish by birth – Israelites who rejected Jesus had betrayed their heritage and scorned their birthright. As a Jew himself, the Seer loved Israel and valued his part in God's Chosen People. What is said in these letters about specific individuals and groups should not be misread as representing an attitude to the Jewish people in general.

have been people who claimed a private secret knowledge that set them apart from ordinary Christians; whoever they were, the Nicolaitans were tearing people away from the truth. The High Priest doesn't blame the churches that such heresies and divisions emerge, but he does inspect the communities to see if they are taking action. It is evident from these letters that authentic teaching about the truths of faith and the moral life is another of the central standards by which the churches are to be judged.

The Key Demand

When we took our imaginary tour of the seven cities of the seven churches, we could see that it made sense to address the first letter to Ephesus and the last one to Laodicea. The order of letters simply follows a very natural route for the messenger to take, especially starting from John's island of Patmos. Yet the first and last letters are different. Parts of them seem to be raising a central point for all the churches, a point so important that it needs to be emphasised at the beginning and end of the series.

Having looked at some of the standards of inspection in the group of seven letters, something might well strike us if we reread the first letter, the one to the church at Ephesus. The church there seems to meet the requirements – it has works, it bears up under outside pressure, it is actively rejecting various groups of false teachers – yet the High Priest threatens it severely. Something more important than any of the other requirements is at stake: the church has left its love behind.

When we turn to the last letter, we find something similar. The church at Laodicea is found to be lukewarm, and it turns the High Priest's stomach. They need to come to Christ again, to find their riches and healing in him. Jesus has been left knocking and calling outside the door. Meanwhile, the Laodicean church is so loud in its deceptive self-praise that there is a danger that no one will hear the voice of the One so desperate to get in.

When we put the picture together, there is no doubt that the essential demand on the churches is a loving, warm relationship to the risen Jesus. This relationship will show itself in the endeavours of living the faith, in enduring the severe hardships that being a disciple can bring and in faithfulness to the teaching of Jesus in matters doctrinal and moral – but, as the church at Ephesus was to hear to its shame, these things mean nothing if love has grown cold. A burnt-out lampstand might even lose its place among the others (2:5).

Beginning a Self-evaluation

There is a need for us all, as Church, to try to listen to a Voice that is definitely speaking, a Voice that John the Seer claims to have heard directly. No one alive today can say exactly how that happened or how an experience like John's can be categorised. The Seer tells us from the very start that his was an experience in the Spirit (1:10) – a comment that should warn us against crudely trying to translate John's experience into terms of our physical, sensory experiences. All we can safely say is that, from the way in which he wrote his book and the force he put into it, John is telling us he knows that what he has written is more than just an expression of *his* opinion. By accepting Revelation as Scripture, the community of faith puts its own stamp of approval on John's claim.

The voice of Jesus, speaking through the Spirit, addresses us from those pages. It spoke directly to seven communities in the first century. Hearing it speak today may involve a bit more reflection, and applying it may be a rather inexact science, but we need to try. What follows is simply an attempt to take a few steps along that path.

The first thing that strikes me is how the standards of Jesus for the churches differ so radically from the way we tend to evaluate a Christian community. Every year, for instance, the Catholic Church authorities produce an annual report that records the percentage of church growth, numbers of religious and clergy, Catholic populations in each nation and so on. I trust that the compilers realise that such figures don't necessarily matter all that much in the eyes of the High Priest. As the saying goes, 'Man counts heads, God counts hearts.' But the temptation is there to go for success, to think in terms of numbers, to look for tangible results.

Oh yes, Christ is looking for an active discipleship – he wants 'works' to be happening. But he often calls us to failure, not success, just as he himself was called to the cross. The marvellously popular religion teacher, the hard-working bishop who manages his diocese well, the mother of a family strongly rooted in the faith have done no more 'works' than the dedicated religion teacher whose classroom life is a drudgery, or than the zealous and caring bishop whose administration is constantly criticised, or than the loving mother whose family – despite her efforts – have all abandoned the Church. In many ways, the last three have received the higher calling. The first three might not have been able to respond to such lofty vocations.

What is true of individual disciples is also true of the Church. We are called to live a public witness which will certainly meet with rejection and resistance from someone, somewhere. Churches should know that they are in trouble if their pronouncements and activities are constantly being praised from all quarters. If we cannot accept that God can be calling us to failure, then we will insist on rewriting the call of God before we answer it.

To take an example, the churches are called to proclaim the Word of God,[8] but not to ensure that it is accepted by those who hear it. In fact, we are actually guaranteed a certain amount of failure in this activity.[9] But when Christian teaching proves unpopular, we feel the temptation to trim it, to leave parts of it unspoken, to make it palatable no matter what the cost. Calls can always be heard for the Church to lower its moral standards or to water down the truths of its faith. So, throughout the centuries, there have been bishops who have blessed horrendous wars instead of proclaiming the gospel of peace, theologians who have loudly denied central truths that happen to be unpopular, and preachers who have avoided proclaiming what they know to be the teaching of the gospel if it touches nerves or lessens the size of their congregations. Some-

---

8. In Catholic tradition, the Word of God is not simply equated with the Scriptures. Because the Scriptures express the Word of God in a thoroughly human expression, the Word must be listened for in the Scriptures. The Word also continues to speak in the living Tradition of the Church, and that too needs listening and interpretation. Fundamentalism and literalist approaches to either Scripture or Tradition deny the incarnational nature of the Word and are repugnant to Catholic belief. In this book, I will retain the capital letter for 'Tradition' whenever I am referring to the living Tradition of the Church that stretches back to its earliest days. When 'tradition' (with a small 't') occurs, it refers to customs and practices that have arisen in time or in only one part of the Church and which do not form part of Tradition as an expression of the Word of God.

9. See Ezekiel 3:4-11, Mark 4:14-20 or John 15:20-21, for example.

times such people succeed in having a quiet life, or keeping their comfort and popularity, or even in making a name for themselves; but the price is failure for the Word of God.

When we look at our own church, whether under the local guise of parish community or as the worldwide community of faith, we must be concerned with its endurance in the midst of trouble, its faithfulness to the truth of Christ and its efforts to put that truth into action. However, if there is one thing that the seven letters tell us needs attention above all, it is the warm, loving relationship to which Jesus insistently calls us. We can gauge how far down the agenda that particular item has slid by our tendency to think of that relationship as private and individual. The letters of Revelation (and most of the New Testament for that matter) speak of this relationship differently: it is one between Jesus and the Church, not one of private devotion. Of course there is a wonderful personal dimension to our relationship with Jesus, but when we gather or act as Church the intimacy of our love should not go into hiding. That relationship should be radiant, consuming and impossible to hide. Outsiders looking at our churches should be left in no doubt that we are people who are in love with the living person of Jesus, not some group that could best be described as, well, lukewarm.

In concentrating on Christ's inspection of the lampstands, I hope that I haven't given the impression that these seven letters are about threat and criticism. If I have, look at them again. You will find that they are filled with the majesty of Christ and the power of his promise. None of the churches, no matter how negative much of its letter seems, is simply dismissed. Each one is offered a reward for responding to the message, a guarantee that its members can inherit the Kingdom Jesus has won for them. If any church, or anyone looking at a church, hasn't been left with a sense of its destiny and dignity as a People called by God, the voice of the Spirit hasn't yet been heard; for the voice of the Spirit is whispering a message of hope and healing, even where the woundedness is greatest.

Questions for Reflection and Prayer

1. Which New Testament images of Church do you find most helpful for shaping an authentic understanding of the Church

today? Which images of Church underlie the Seer's choice of addressing his message to seven Christian communities in Asia Minor?

2. Given the obvious shortcomings and limitations of the Church, is it surprising that John can still present Christ as identified with his Church, and that he loves it tenderly like a spouse?

3. What common concerns emerge in the seven letters to the churches. Can these concerns have meaning for Christians today?

4. How can churches today hear the Spirit's message? What do you reckon might be among the key demands for the Church today?

3

The Throne Room of the King

Revelation 4:1 – 5:14

If someone living in Dublin wants to escape for the day, all they have to do is head northwards towards the Boyne Valley. Apart from the beautiful countryside, there are plenty of sites worth a visit. I've made the tour or parts of it dozens of times and never been disappointed. Among my favourite places to visit are the five-thousand year old burial mounds of Knowth and Newgrange, the royal ceremonial Hill of Tara that was in use two thousand years ago and the ancient monastic ruins of Monasterboice and Mellifont. These historic remains all bear witness to one fact: even though they belong to different ages and cultures, they all give testimony to the human desire to worship. Each one was a centre for ceremony and ritual. In each place, human hearts tried to reach to something beyond.

Can we speak of a human need to worship? Perhaps we can, as long as we allow worshipping to be as wide-ranging a term as knowing. We all know people who show no more need to worship than they do to go mountain-climbing. But on the other hand we see the unbounded devotion and celebration that can surround music groups and football teams. Even political ideas have inspired songs and rallies that celebrate deep loyalties and commitments to something beyond the individual. Worship may not be the first word that springs to mind, but something of it is there.

The Sunday Routine

Sunday after Sunday, Christians gather for their particular forms of worship. They forge another link in a chain that has been growing without a break for over two thousand years. The ceremonies once performed at Newgrange and the Hill of Tara have long since fallen from the memory but, ever since Jesus made his request, 'Do this in memory of me,' the Breaking of the Bread has never stopped. And it never will.

Despite this unity of practice spanning the centuries, a sample from the congregation of any Sunday Eucharist would probably represent as many different reasons for being there as there are people in the sample. I belong to the generation of 'You have to go to Mass on Sunday' Catholics. Although we were given some fine reasons for going to Mass when we were taught about the Eucharist, there seemed to be more emphasis in the Church of the 1950s on the obligation and the consequence of breaking it. The commandment to 'Keep holy the Sabbath' was heard first and foremost – and mistakenly – in many a Catholic ear as a commandment to go to Mass. When you lived, as my family did, several miles from the church, there was also the worry about how late you could be before you had to go to a second Mass or how sick you had to feel before you didn't have to go to Mass at all. Priests had to ensure that the first Masses of Christmas and Easter didn't begin before the stroke of midnight so that the obligation would be sure to be fulfilled. It was a different age and a commandment was reason enough on its own.

The obligation mentality still influences some people strongly, but it is no longer the ready answer it once was. There can still be powerful family and social pressures to attend Mass, so some members of the congregation will be in the church to keep their parents happy (or at least quiet), or to be seen, or to meet the neighbours. Then there are other reasons; I once heard a young girl say that she would never miss Mass because, if she did, she wouldn't have any luck for the week!

Apart from a variety of reasons, there are also different ways of taking part. Some get involved in reading, leading prayers or singing in choirs. Others actively listen to the readings, pray the responses and sing the hymns as ordinary members of the congregation while still others prefer to concentrate more on their private prayer than on the community aspect of worship. Others are just there, saying nothing, singing nothing and thinking their own thoughts. If we were honest, there has probably been some time or other that we fitted most neatly into this group, even if it were just for a few minutes. We would be wrong to think that worship is totally meaningless for such people, even though we ourselves might have found more meaning in our own manner of participation. Years ago a priest friend of mine was teaching in a school and the subject of discussion was going to Mass on Sundays. One of the students became quite heated in the debate, giving out about the laziness of those who couldn't be bothered getting up and going to Mass on a Sunday morning. My friend couldn't restrain himself. He said to the young fellow, 'Look, I say Mass in your parish every Sunday and I know your story. You never come into the church. You stay outside with your pals and kick a football against the church wall and distract everybody inside!' 'Yes,' the student answered, 'but at least I go!' – and he was being serious.

Of course there are many reasons for not joining the congregation on Sunday and most of us have heard them all (and could add to them ourselves): Mass is boring. I can't understand the readings. The sermon is drivel. Our priest takes too long. The young priest rushes through everything. The choir is horrible. The church is cold. The church is too hot. That Eucharistic minister is a hypocrite. The whole congregation are hypocrites. They ruined the church when they remodelled it. The priests are always looking for money. Sunday is my only day for a lie-in.

Most of us, I think, could find something in that list to agree with. But there must be something else, something that sweeps the objections aside like so much dust on a valuable piece of furniture. And I don't think that a sense of Sunday obligation is really the answer. Even though we may have our own approaches and good reasons for our worship, the section of Revelation that forms the basis of this chapter might provide us with a bit more to think about.

On the Lord's Day

To understand the Apocalypse, we have to keep referring back to what John tells us at the very beginning. We have already noted part of 1:10 where the author tells us that he was in the Spirit; but the next phrase is equally significant: he informs us that this happened 'on the Lord's Day.'

The Seer thought it important enough to make the connection for his audience between what he experienced and the day of the week on which it happened. Because we don't know exactly what the Seer's circumstances were, we can only guess what was the link exactly. We would be mistaken to think that Sunday was a day of rest for John as it is for modern Christians and that the vision happened during some imagined Sabbath quiet time; in a world run by worshippers of Zeus and Apollo, Sunday was as much a working day as any other. What characterised Sunday for early Christians was worship and the Eucharist, and the link is undoubtedly to be found there. If John were with other Christians on Patmos, as would seem probable, he seems to be saying that he had his experience in the Spirit either while participating in the community's worship or as an aftereffect of his worship. In the less likely event that John was isolated from a worshipping community, the connection might be found in his own prayer on that day made in a union of spirits with the community with which he was longing to worship.

We know that worship was very important to John from the way he uses it in his book. We have already seen him drawing images from his fond memories of joining in the worship of the Jerusalem Temple. In Revelation 4-5, he brings us further into the heavenly Temple and draws us deeper into that worship.

Entering the Awesome Sanctuary

The very act of going to the Temple was quite different from the act of going to church today. Most of us actually enter the church, take our seats and the liturgy takes place in our presence and with our participation. In contrast, going to the Jerusalem Temple did not mean entering the Temple building, or Sanctuary, itself.[1] The vast majority of worshippers stayed in the courts surrounding the Sanctuary. As a non-Jew I would have had to stay in the largest court which was also the one most removed from the Sanctuary. There were large notices to remind people like me that going any further would mean the death penalty under the Law of Israel. All Israelites could enter the next court, the Court of the Women. This was a spacious area and some of the ceremonies took place here. Male Israelites could go a little further, up fifteen steps into the smaller Court of the Israelites. Only priests and Levites[2] could enter

1. The New Testament uses one word to speak of the Temple building itself and another to speak of the whole Temple complex, including the courts. When the gospels speak of Jesus going to the Temple, they use the word for the Temple complex, but when the Fourth Gospel speaks of Jesus' body as the new Temple, it uses the word for the Temple building itself. Translations differ in the way that they translate these two words. I will keep the word 'Sanctuary' as a term for the actual Temple building, the House of God.

2. Priests and Levites were the liturgical functionaries of the Temple and they were all members of the tribe of Levi. Religious duties made a full-time occupation for only

the court immediately surrounding the Sanctuary, the Court of the Priests, where the great altar stood before the Temple building. The Sanctuary itself was considered the House of God, and no one entered it unless the liturgical rites required him to do so. Even within that building there was a section that was more awesome still, the Holy of Holies. No ordinary priest entered this sacred place, only the High Priest alone once a year on the Day of Atonement. The Holy of Holies was the throne room of God on earth, God's presence was somehow there,[3] and human feet were not permitted to enter it.

The Temple complex symbolised in stone an idea that is quite different from our normal way of thinking. Whereas we often blend the sacred and the ordinary, the Hebrew word for 'holy' means 'separate' and holiness could be shown by physically separating what was holy from what was not. The phrase 'Holy of Holies' could possibly also be translated as 'The Most Separated Place'. By protecting the Sanctuary with courts, restrictions and rituals, Israel was showing its deep reverence for their God, their awareness that God is always totally other, even in the very place where Yahweh promises to dwell with humanity. We can still see the ripples of this idea in our own actions: after we consecrate cups and plates for use in the Eucharist, we would never think of using them as ordinary cups and plates. They have been set apart; as an ancient Hebrew would say, they are holy.

The Seer's vision of Jesus the High Priest has already brought him past all of the courts and the altar and into the heavenly Sanctuary lit by its sacred lampstands. John saw into a place so holy that few would have ever even been able to glance into its mere earthly counterpart in Jerusalem. He would have been painfully

---

a very few 'chief' priests. Scattered wherever Israelites were to be found, ordinary priests came and served at the Temple for a week according to a rota. Levites were the non-priestly members of the tribe who assisted the priests and shared in some of their privileges; they had a special responsibility for the ceremonial music, among other things.

3. Scripture is very careful to avoid speaking of God's presence in the Temple as if it were a crude physical presence. The Hebrew Bible speaks of God's glory or God's name dwelling in the Temple to express a presence that we might think of as unique and sacramental. Later Jewish writing (after biblical times) sometimes uses the word *shekina* (or 'that which dwells') to differentiate between the very person of Yahweh and the manner in which the Divine was present in the Temple.

aware that he had no right to be there. As if that were not enough, John tells us that a door opened in heaven and that he was invited into the Holy of Holies in heaven itself. This invitation must have struck terror into the Seer's heart. After all, the Scriptures often echo the Israelite belief that to look upon the face of God was to die. Other nations all had their idols, but the God of Israel was unseen. In Solomon's ancient temple, the Ark of the Covenant acted as a footstool for Yahweh's unseen presence. Pagans found this hard to take; how could you have a god that you couldn't represent with gold, silver or stone? But the faith of Israel knew better. God always remains beyond both human imaging and imagining.

The Seer Sets the Scene

The Hebrew Bible does record visions of Yahweh, but always with great caution, always sending out signals that the prophet has only seen a small part and that the words, try as they might, keep failing to get even that small part across. There is never an attempt to tell us what God looks like, just an account of what it was to be swept into the divine presence. 'This is only a vision,' each one seems to say, 'not the reality.' Two of these visions were precisely of the Temple presence of Yahweh, and John the Seer has used their imagery to describe his own experience on the Lord's Day.

The first comes from Isaiah 6:1-5. Isaiah seems to have found himself at the Jerusalem Temple which as a pious Israelite he would always have acknowledged to be the House of Yahweh. But then something happened. Instead of the dwelling of Yahweh in the Temple being just a truth of Isaiah's faith affirmed by the mind, it became an experience affecting the whole person:

> I saw my Lord sitting on a throne, exalted, lifted up, and the hem of his garment filled the Temple building! Fiery beings[4] were in attendance from above, six wings for each of them – each covered its face with two wings, each covered its feet with two wings and each used two wings for flying. They cried out to one another: 'Holy! Holy! Holy is Yahweh Sabaoth! The whole world is filled with his Glory!'

To Isaiah's surprise, the first thing that the vision communicates

---

4. The Hebrew word used here gives us the English word 'seraphim'.

The Throne Room of the King (Rev 4:1-5:14)

is that the Temple is far too small. What Israel called the 'House of Yahweh' couldn't even contain the hem of God's garment. As for the practice of speaking of the glory of Yahweh dwelling in the Temple as a way of admitting the Temple's limitations – why even Yahweh's glory fills the whole world!

The other vision is also of the glory of Yahweh, that is, God's Temple presence – but it took place hundreds of miles from the Temple building. While the prophet Ezekiel and the people with him were in exile from Jerusalem and the land of Israel, one of their great sorrows was being unable to draw near God in the Temple. At the beginning of the book that bears his name, Ezekiel relates how he was stunned to see God's glory drawing near him instead. The visual language that Ezekiel uses is forceful and seems to tie itself, its images and its readers into knots, but the prophet shows us the throne of God's glory streaming with fire and lightning, with fiery beings with the faces of humans, lions, oxen and eagles in attendance. If you look at the passage, you will see that words are failing Ezekiel. Words were never made that could take the strain of expressing what Ezekiel tells us is only 'a likeness of the glory of Yahweh' (Ezek 1:28); the idea of looking upon Yahweh's very self would definitely have been out of the question for Ezekiel.

Since Isaiah and Ezekiel are two books that the Seer often alludes to throughout the Apocalypse, it is not surprising that parts of these two visions have been used by John to communicate his own. In Revelation 4:2-8 we meet again with the faces of the humans and beasts Ezekiel told us of, and we hear echoed the strains of the 'Holy, Holy, Holy' described by Isaiah. Like Isaiah and Ezekiel, the Seer tells us that he is describing a visionary experience, not the fullness of a reality that eyes cannot see nor ears hear. Yet the Seer's vision goes beyond the claims of the two ancient prophets: this is not a revelation of the divine presence in the earthly Temple, but of the divine presence truly at home in the heavenly Temple!

The Scene Moves into Action

John does not paint a frozen tableau for us, but a scene filled with action – and the action is worship. Just as familiar images from Isaiah and Ezekiel helped John's churches to comprehend the overall impact of his vision, images and actions from their experiences of worship helped them to share his understanding of what was going on during this glimpse into heaven. Even though our own experiences of liturgies differ in many ways from John's, we can immediately recognise some of the gestures and acclamations narrated in these chapters as ones that would be at home in many a worshipping community.

The presence and actions of the twenty-four elders would have reminded John's communities of their past worship in the Jerusalem Temple. The number twenty-four is especially significant. Week by week, a different division of priests served in the temple but, at the great festivals, all twenty-four divisions were called into action. The presence of twenty-four elders (an honorific term sometimes used for priests in the ancient world)[5] dressed in the white garments of the Israelite priesthood give the vision a special solemnity; these heavenly figures represent the full priesthood present for a festive liturgy, not just the section that would be responsible for a morning or evening service on an ordinary day. Other elements of this picture belong to the liturgies of Israel's great feasts: the priests wore crowns in the Temple at the feast of Tabernacles and made a great solemn prostration on the Day of Atonement. John is telling us that we have been brought past the joy and solemnity of the most memorable ceremony anyone could ever remember in Jerusalem (and all the evidence goes to prove that they were memorable) into the great unceasing festival of heaven itself.

At the time Revelation was written John's communities could no longer go to the Jerusalem Temple; it had been tragically destroyed in the Jewish war with Rome years before. Fond as their memories were of the splendours of those ancient liturgies, these early disciples had an act of worship that far surpassed the Temple rites in meaning, if not in ceremony. The Seer seems to have drawn from that experience too. The arrangement of God's throne flanked by the living creatures and surrounded by elders matches what we know was the arrangement of clergy in some early Christian celebrations: the chair of the bishop flanked by deacons and surrounded by concelebrating elders. Most of the existing evidence

---

5. The Greek word for 'elder' gives us the English word 'presbyter' and, over time, the word 'priest'.

indicates that the triple cry of 'Holy' in various forms was an important congregational acclamation in the earliest Eucharistic Liturgies of the Church; if this were the custom for John and his communities, the cries of the four living creatures provide another strong link between the vision and their experience of Eucharistic worship.

Such details and connections are only indicators to John's deeper insight. The Seer is telling his audience that what they do week by week in their worship is, in fact, a dim reflection in time and space of something that is really happening in the splendour and majesty and eternity of the heavenly Sanctuary, just as that Sanctuary once had an earthly symbol of itself in the Jerusalem Temple. The liturgies of John's communities were probably not very splendid; they would have known nothing of the vestments, incense and great choral music that were to come in later centuries. The major decoration of these liturgies would have been (as it still should be) the love and commitment of the worshipping churches, but we have already been told that some had left their love behind and others had grown lukewarm. Over the years some members of the Seer's churches had undoubtedly already let their appreciation of worship fade and they were participating more or less because of routine. By sketching this picture of heaven with lines borrowed from the early Eucharist, John gives his readers a humbling and stunning revelation: in the liturgies of the churches, unimpressive as they may be, mere humans are privileged to join in the very industry of heaven – the celebration and worship that belongs to the celestial beings when they are in the fullest presence of God.

The Presentation of the Sacrifice

Modern Christians are well used to speaking of Jesus as the Lamb of God. For many, I am sure, the phrase captures something of the innocence and gentleness that they associate with Jesus – and these are associations that are truly appropriate to this biblical description. But we can't stop there when we read the Apocalypse.

John uses the title of 'lamb' for Jesus over twenty-five times in Revelation, nearly three times as often as we find the more familiar title 'Christ' in the book. The first time the image is used is in Revelation 5:6:

I saw in the middle of the throne and of the four living beings and in the middle of the elders a lamb that was in attendance as one that had been slain. The lamb had seven horns and seven eyes, these being the seven spirits of God sent out into all the world.

The reference to the Lamb having been slain makes a central point about why Jesus is referred to in this way in the Apocalypse. For the Seer, the image of lamb was primarily that of a sacrificial animal – as it was for all of the New Testament writers – and John's use of the image will draw our thoughts to various aspects of the sacrifice of Jesus and the consequences of that offering.

Sacrifices have always played a special part in human worship, even though they take different forms and shapes. Through their sacrifices, people hope that something valuable from their own world will be accepted into the world of the divine and somehow unlock blessings that are beyond mere human achievement. Sacrifices can be made in different ways: slaughtering an animal, pouring out a liquid onto the ground or the altar, and burning incense are some of the more familiar examples. We often think of the holocaust (in which the animal is completely consumed by fire) as a typical sacrifice but it was not the only one in use in Israel. In the Law of Moses, there were various reasons given for sacrifice and appropriate rituals prescribed for different occasions. The Passover Lamb, for instance, was seen as a sacrificial meal to be shared between Yahweh and the household that offered it. The blood of the Lamb was given to God while the flesh of the Lamb was eaten by the household at a celebratory meal. Many of the sacrificial rituals reflected this deep bonding between the people of Israel and their God. Other sacrifices were offered for thanksgiving, for praise, for purification or for forgiveness.

Since New Testament times, Christians have used the language of sacrifice to speak of various acts of offering to God. St Paul, for instance, can speak of the whole self-outpouring of his ministry, the gifts sent to support him and the Christian's day-to-day dedication of the whole person to God all as sacrifices.[6] We continue to use such language today when we speak of 'offering up' something that we would like to avoid but which must be endured. But we all know

6. See Philippians 2:17, Philippians 4:18 and Romans 12:1.

that, strictly speaking, there is only one real sacrifice for Christians, only one act that has pierced the heavens and unlocked the blessings of love, mercy and forgiveness, and that is the sacrifice of the Lamb. John places a unique concentration on this sacrifice and shows us how wide-ranging the effects of that great act of worship really are.

John makes it clear that the Lamb of Revelation is no ordinary sacrificial lamb. He is first announced as Lion, not Lamb, and hailed as a conqueror (5:5); nor has the Seer forgotten his vision of Jesus as High Priest. The Lamb presents himself to the One Seated on the Throne (5:5-7) and so shows himself to be both priest and victim;[7] the Lamb is not only the sacrificial victim, but the one who presents the sacrifice. Most surprising of all, John shows us that the Lamb belongs to a league of offering totally different to anything Israel had ever sacrificed before. Most sacrifices can be thought of as taking something that is mine and giving it to God. This is not true of the Lamb. The divinity of the Lamb is shown in many ways in this text: he is to be found in the middle of God's throne;[8] he has seven horns, the fullest sign of divinity;[9] he has the seven eyes that belong to God and the sevenfold Spirit of God;[10] he is the object of hymns in the heavenly Sanctuary; finally, and most significantly, the Lamb is worshipped together with the One on the throne. The Lamb is a divine sacrifice. Humanity has not given something totally of its own to God, but the divine Lamb alone has given the sacrifice that will change the world. The Seer, who has been privileged to view the liturgy of its presentation, now begins to unfold it for us.

---

7. John is not so tied to the concrete details or possible consequences of his imagery that he draws back from the tensions that he creates when he blends them – such as the tensions we might feel here when lion, lamb and priest are all mixed together. This approach of John's can sometimes make us uncomfortable with his images or even confuse us; what we call 'mixed metaphors' sometimes give us mental indigestion. We can avoid that feeling by trying to concentrate only on those aspects of the images on which the Seer is focusing our attention and putting the seeming contradictions to one side for the moment.

8. This is the most obvious way to read the Greek of 5:6. Some translations place the Lamb between the throne and the elders in an attempt to make sense of a difficult Greek construction.

9. The ram's horn was sometimes used as a symbol of divinity. Alexander the Great was depicted on a coin with a ram's horn for precisely this reason.

10. See Zechariah 4:10 for the reference to the seven eyes of God.

The Effects of Worship

Just for the moment, let us forget about the scenes we are being shown in Revelation and return to thinking about our own experience of worship. When we try to put words on the effects of worship, what terms do we come up with? We might speak of strength to live the Christian life, or renewal of our relationship with God. Some might express the same ideas with an older phrase like 'increase of grace'. The focus is still the same: worship, when it works properly, does something primarily for the worshipper.

Revelation shows us a radically different perspective with its introduction of the scroll with seven seals. This scroll, so crammed that the writing fills both sides, is nothing less than the plan of God for history. But there is a problem: this mysterious and glorious blueprint cannot be executed. It is sealed seven times over, and there is no one able to open the seals. No wonder the Seer breaks down and cries. All of the promises of God, all of the hopes of Israel, all possibility that goodness will ever triumph over injustice, hatred and bloodshed lie unrealised under the strength of those unbreakable seals.

All of that changes through the power of worship. The sacrifice of the Lamb rightly raises the strains of rejoicing in the heavenly Sanctuary, for it means that the seals can be loosened and the great plan of God can begin to reveal itself in history. Worship is not just about my individual relationship to God or getting my prayers answered or fulfilling some basic human need. Worship joins the Lamb in transforming history, challenging the grip of sin and evil, welcoming the Kingdom. Worship, as we shall see, is nothing less than world-shattering, the action of God accompanied by the shouts of blessing, honour, glory and power that cannot possibly be suppressed in the mouths of God's People.

It would not be an exaggeration to speak of the rest of the narrative of the Apocalypse as a presentation of the consequences of the Lamb's sacrifice, as an unfolding and implementation of the scroll that only this heavenly liturgy could unseal. In that sense, the great liturgy described to us in these chapters dominates John's book. The Seer has not finished with his portrayal of worship, nor with his presentation of its place and meaning, but even at this point he has given us a different perspective to think about.

The Throne Room of the King (Rev 4:1-5:14)

We should begin with the very notion of a heavenly liturgy, performed as it is by the angelic choirs. Admittedly, many Christians are not quite comfortable with talking about angels. There is definitely a feeling that a belief in angels is somewhat theologically unsophisticated. Perhaps this is the unfortunate result of some past theologians (who would have considered themselves *very* sophisticated) going overboard in defining, describing, ranking and enumerating angelic beings as if they were producing an inventory of some type of supernatural produce for stocktaking. But when you put that sort of thing aside, what you end up with from the Scriptures and Christian Tradition are lovely pictures of God's protection, of unseen gratuitous friendships whose sole object is to lead us to God, of a gracefulness and power that cannot be totally captured by the human mind and senses, of songs of God's glory that cannot be surpassed or stopped, of a Creator who does not just create the necessary and pragmatic but the wondrous and beautiful as well, of a universe in which humanity is not always the most mysterious or important thing around. Given all of that, any theology that excludes angels is drab, prosaic, puritanical – and ultimately unsophisticated, for it shows its basic inability to appreciate anything beyond the narrow limits of its own logic.

Christian Tradition has always insisted that what it does in its liturgy, especially in the Eucharistic Liturgy, borrows from the angels and joins an action that is happening constantly in heaven. The liturgy is not just something we do ourselves in our own congregations at this particular time in this particular place; we are united to an act that is so great that mere time and space cannot contain it. However we express this in words and ideas, the transcendental aspect of worship easily slips from the worshipper's mind and, when it does, our congregations can allow their horizons to collapse in upon themselves. The act of worship all of a sudden belongs wholly to the people who plan it, perform it and participate in it; there is no longer an awareness of the privilege we have to be a small moving part in a vast action that the whole Church – seen and unseen – joyfully makes before God. We begin to limit our prayers of intercession to ourselves and the people we know. Our sense of awe before the living God shrivels and our awareness of the risen Jesus becomes more theoretical than experienced. If we do not strongly link in some way our theology and practice of church worship to its transcendental dimension, we can expect growing difficulties to emerge in forming and nurturing that essential aspect of Christian life and vision that views all things in the light of the Wholly Other and acts accordingly.

The Seer's vision of the celestial worship makes no mention of his seven churches, but it tells them in a different way who they are and what they do: they are concelebrants with the Lamb and angels and saints; they are part of a royal priesthood chosen to celebrate the glory of God. Their humble and stumbling attempts to worship are made stunning and glorious by their seamless link with the choirs of heaven and the priestly ministry of Christ. John is telling us that, unless we see in liturgy the earthly Church joined to heaven and heaven embracing the earthly Church, we have not begun to understand what the Church's worship really is.

Even this presentation of John's vision could be accused of being too static. Something happens in the Seer's heavenly liturgy; through it the plan of God unfolds. As we read through Revelation, we will get a sense that this is also part of the way the Seer views the earthly Church's liturgies. Liturgy is not something to be done in isolation just for its own sake for whatever reason we can tag onto it. The Church's communal worship in some way participates in the unfolding of God's design and the shaping of history.

Because the liturgy is inseparable from the sacrifice of the Lamb, it is only through worship that we can join in breaking those seals that prevent God's will and plan taking shape in our world. All the toils and struggles we make in response to the gospel and the needs of others, all our planned programmes and individual actions can remain isolated and futile – just a series of temporary failures and successes that will be forgotten in the sweep of history. But when these are joined to the sacrificial worship led by the Lamb, each becomes part of the great pageant of triumph that will open the plan of God and reveal the Kingdom.

The Seer was no composer of rubrics. He has not laid down an order of service or told us how to vest our elders or arrange their chairs. Instead, he has proposed a reason for our worship as Church by showing the realities that lie at its heart. John's insight should produce a sense of compulsion that makes the Sunday obligation pale by comparison: if Christians want to do something practical, they must take their part in the great symphony raised in heaven and on earth to God and the Lamb, and then things will really begin to happen.

Only the Seer went through that door opened for him in heaven and the vision was given to him alone. However, when the Church's worship becomes earthbound, when the angels' voices are not even faintly heard, when stock prayers become a monotonous recitation, and the cries of 'Glory' a routine murmur, the Spirit is still inviting the churches to lift up their eyes a bit, at least to try catching a glimpse of what John saw. If we do, we – as individuals and as churches – will have our own small experiences of being in the Spirit on the Lord's Day, very different from John's, but real and memorable all the same.

Questions for Reflection and Prayer

1. What links can be made between the importance worship held for the Seer as illustrated in Revelation 4-5 and our understanding of worship today?

2. John's insights on worship should produce a sense of compulsion that makes the 'Sunday obligation' pale by comparison. What are the implications of this for your participation in worship?

3. How does the Seer attempt to encourage the churches in their weekly worship? How does it surpass the Temple rites in meaning? What meaning can this have for our liturgies today?

4. John uses the title of Lamb for Jesus over twenty-five times in Revelation, thereby emphasising the sacrificial aspect to Jesus' self-giving. How can modern Christians enter more fully into this symbolism and allow it influence their participation in Eucharistic worship?

4

Disturbing Sounds of Breaking Seals and Blaring Trumpets

Revelation 6:1 – 9:21

Sometimes those who study the Apocalypse are puzzled by the fact that, in Revelation 5:5, a lion is announced but a lamb appears. I think far more of us are bewildered that the Lamb acts more like a lion, despite his sheeplike appearance.

In this section of the Apocalypse we come face to face with that aspect of the book that causes problems for so many of its readers. Why does all of this destruction appear in the Seer's book? Why does he recount it in such horrific detail? Is it really necessary – is it really Christian?

If we feel overwhelmed at the sound of the hoofbeats that signal the advance of the four dread horsemen, it is because the Seer wants us to be overwhelmed. If we are confused at the sudden and devastating appearance of war, famine and death, it could be because John has given us no reason to expect them. Part (and only part) of our negative reaction on reading this text is totally in keeping with what the author expects us to feel. He consciously creates a contrast between the glory and splendour of God's throne room and the horror of the events that he tells us are about to take place on earth.

World without End?

In the early 1990s, an astronomer calculated that an asteroid's orbit would bring it into collision with the earth with disastrous results. His calculations were announced with a precise year, month and day given for the devastation of the planet. When I first read the news item, I misread the figure and understood that the scientist seemed to be predicting an event early in the twenty-first century. A quick second look brought me a sigh of relief, for the suggested timing was actually in the twenty-second century. The one, I thought, I might be around for, but not the second.

Even my self-centred gut reaction doesn't totally remove the tinge of sadness at the prospect of such a calamity for our planet. I was delighted to hear that the experts found errors in the prediction. This collision will not take place. There is so much beauty and goodness about the earth and the delicate web of life it supports; any event that would seriously damage all this wonder must be seen as a senseless tragedy by any human person.

So how can I not have problems reading this section of Revelation? It seems to go against so much of the celebration of the goodness of creation that we find in the Scriptures. An initial encounter with this part of the Apocalypse will produce little evidence of that positive, world-affirming Christian outlook that sees the presence and action of God in ordinary reality, both as created and as enhanced by human endeavour. We find it hard to reconcile the visionary events here described with the call spoken with such urgency by theologians, scientists and the churches to be loving and responsible stewards of the earth. If we have to make a choice, most of us would quickly put this part of Revelation into the background and think happier thoughts instead. I know that is my tendency.

By doing so, I could be fooling myself on a number of counts. I could be pretending that the world will go on forever. It won't. It is totally dependent upon a neighbouring star that will eventually die and take the planet with it. All right, that's millions of years away, but let's not quibble about numbers. On this point science and religion agree: the world was never made to be eternal.

I could also be playing the ostrich, ignoring the fact that catastrophic tragedies actually occur in the real world – or I could be pretending that they wouldn't if people like the Seer didn't talk about them. I have a childhood recollection of hiding under a cinema seat during a frightening scene in a film, not protecting myself from a monster that might get me but from the *knowledge* that the monster was there. That cowering child is still part of me and resents it when John and his kind will not let me cringe into my own comfort of denial. If you must tell me about tragedies, then add quickly that science or relief agencies or *someone* will soon have the thing under control. If I must acknowledge the reality of suffering, at least let me think of it as partial, temporary and solvable.

Then too, I might be unfairly putting too much blame on the Seer for presenting something that I don't like. I certainly am if I think this whole idea of the world coming to an end, or that tragedy and calamity can be part of God's plan, started with John. Such notions were there well before John; they cannot simply be removed from the biblical totality without doing some serious structural damage. The roots of these ideas can be found in the prophetic awareness that God's action not only brings the good gifts of creation but that God is also free to withdraw or destroy such gifts if the greater good of Israel demands it.[1] Faith in Yahweh's lordship over both creation and Israel celebrates the wonders of creation and Yahweh's mighty deeds in history in many biblical texts. It is this same awareness of Yahweh's lordship that permits the prophets to see God's action even in tragedy.

We can hardly fail to notice that the passing nature of this world is evident in the preaching of Jesus in the gospels. There we are told that this world will dramatically end amidst many trials and catastrophes to make room for the Kingdom of the Messiah, and that this is Good News not bad.[2] What the Seer has to say about the world's demise is part of the Christian message; as a disciple I must eventually come to terms with it. I am not really free to mentally brush the whole notion of a passing world out of sight just because I don't like the way in which John has expressed it.

The real blind spot behind my instant inclination to put these chapters aside could arise from recognising creation's goodness and wonder without acknowledging that God has planned a greater

---

1. Although the Hebrew Bible often uses the metaphor of punishment in these passages, an attentive reading shows that the divine intention is to produce a return to God. Harsh and threatening as these texts might seem, they embody an invitation and an opportunity that other methods have failed to communicate. Among passages where this can be seen are Hosea 2:1-20 (where Israel is represented as the unfaithful spouse of Yahweh), Joel 2:3-14 and Amos 5:1-6.

2. This teaching is particularly evident in what are termed 'the apocalyptic discourses' of the gospels; when reading them, one must remember that they, like the Book of Revelation, are written as apocalyptic literature and that what is said in the Introduction about interpreting such writing applies to these passages too. Even an initial reading will show that the emphasis in these passages is not on the details of the end of the world, but on how disciples should act in the light of the knowledge that the world will pass away and that Jesus will return as judge. See Mark 13:1-37, Matthew 24:1-25:46 and Luke 21:5-36. Another early apocalyptic text can be found in 2 Thessalonians 2:1-15.

goodness and wonder still. I forget that, for the original audiences, the apocalyptic passages of the New Testament inspired hope, not despair. I can only share the comfort the original audiences derived from these texts insofar as I share their yearning for the fullness of the Kingdom that only the Second Coming of Jesus will bring. During Advent, every time I pray the ancient cry of the Church, 'Maranatha – O Lord, come!' something in me mumbles, 'But not yet' – and that something holds me back from really appreciating the Good News that even these chapters of Revelation contain.

The plagues of Revelation 6-9 are given only as a foreshadowing of the end of the world; the end itself comes later in the book. Even so, considering this section gives us a chance to put the negative aspect of the Apocalypse into perspective. The perspective begins to form when we stop focusing on our gut reaction to these texts and concentrate instead on certain points that were important to John and that we still affirm when we recite the creed: first, this world will not last forever; second, Jesus will come again to judge the living and the dead; third, the Kingdom, which will be fully revealed at the end of the world and the coming of Jesus, represents the ultimate goal of all God's work, including creation itself.

Not one of these points contradicts a sense of thanksgiving for the gifts of creation. Not one undermines the authentic celebration and enjoyment of the goodness of life. Not one negates the urgency of such things as responsible stewardship of the earth or efforts at putting the Kingdom's values to work, even in a passing world. Keeping these three points in mind should help us to be more in tune with the Seer's perception, even if they don't give us total ease in reading certain parts of his work.

The Beginning of the Great Exodus

In fact, the Seer doesn't seem to want his audience to be all that comfortable at the beginning of chapter six. He paints such black pictures that very little light shines through them. The only indication that there is something positive about what is happening at the appearance of the four horsemen is that they come as the result of the sacrifice, their coming is somehow part of the great plan of God and therefore must be accepted, even if with a trembling heart.

The Seer is not the first biblical writer to speak of catastrophe as part of the working out of the divine plan. One of the earliest and most memorable series of such disasters was the ten plagues inflicted on Egypt. They would have been a familiar part of what everyone knew about the story of Israel. They were recounted at table every Passover, but not as part of a tragic tale. They were part of the story of the triumph of God and the saving of Israel. Freeing the Chosen People was a momentous business that required dramatic measures. If the price hadn't been paid, the prize would not have been won.

John draws from the story of the ten plagues with good reason. He, too, is telling the story of a liberation of God's People. If the price seems higher, the prize is much greater as well.

The Seer introduces us to the People of God for the first time in chapter seven. Like the ancient Hebrew families protected from the angel of death's descent in Egypt, these are people who have been sealed and protected by the blood of the Lamb. Firstly, they are spoken of as Israel. We should not imagine that John is talking just of those who are physically descended from the Israelite nation. His picture in 7:4-8 has restored the lost tribes and uses multiples of Israel's special symbolic number twelve to convey an Israel brought to perfection, the Chosen People as desired by God.

The listing of the tribes was given in a report that John heard. When he actually sees this Chosen People take their place in the heavenly liturgy, things appear quite different. The symbolic nature of the figure of 144,000 becomes clear at once, for no one could find the numbers to count this group. They may all have been given their places among Israel and its tribes, but they represent the whole world and all its peoples. These are the Israel now being liberated, the ones for whose sake everything happens. They are in festive dress and festive spirit as they join in the celestial worship in 7:9-12. Their white garments and palm branches belong to the great feast of Tabernacles, the greatest and most joyous festival in the calendar of the Jerusalem Temple. The worship of this people is so enthusiastic that even angels have to take second place in the liturgy, putting their 'Amen' to the shouts of those in white robes.

When we focus on this vision of God's People, we should begin to understand the horrors that the Seer relates are part of the story of triumph and liberation. If the scenes are terrifying, they are not as horrendous as the prospect that God's People would remain unredeemed. John's communities were well aware that they were not exempt from their own trials and tribulations as the great scroll of God's plan opens. They are called to share in suffering and they need heroic endurance; but, despite appearances, they are sealed by the Lamb's sacrifice, clothed in garments washed by his blood, and promised that their every tear will be wiped away.

The Seven Trumpets

It is understandable that people read the catastrophic scenes of these chapters as a description of the end of the world, but John did not write them as such. Even though we are left with an impression of massive destruction, the Seer keeps reminding us that much is spared and only a fraction of the world has been harmed. John has just begun to unfold his story. At most, these catastrophes are only the beginning of the end.

When the seven seals are broken and the scroll fully unrestrained, there is a silence in heaven before the next series of events begins in 8:1-2. John uses that silence to tell us that everything on the opened scroll isn't going to be shown to us quite yet.³ We aren't really ready to view whatever it is that God has planned as the goal and climax of the human story. We still have much to be shown about the world and the working out of God's plan before we can appreciate the finale that the breaking of the seventh seal heralds.

Of course, in these chapters we are still witnessing the heavenly liturgy through John's eyes and John continues to draw from the imagery and language of worship. Of all the musical instruments of the ancient world, the trumpet had the most meaningful associations for Israel. For John, the word would have immediately conjured up pictures of the ram's horn which is hardly the picture

---

3. Something similar happens with the sounding of the seventh trumpet in 11:15 when the full coming of the Kingdom is proclaimed – but not yet shown to John's audience. Many experts in the Book of Revelation suggest that the various sets of seven catastrophes in the book are intended to show the one picture of tribulation from different perspectives rather than a series of consecutive sevens. The fact that the plagues in different sets sometimes echo one another makes this a reasonable approach. In any event, it should be evident by now that John was not trying to be a first century Nostradamus. He is interpreting a whole side of human experience, not cataloguing the details of the experience itself.

that springs to our minds when we hear the word 'trumpet'. The ram's horn was used in ancient Israel to send clear and urgent signals; in time of war especially it was used to sound an alarm. In the liturgy the ram's horn also sounded the alarm of an urgent call to repentance, as Joel 2:1-2 shows. Its blasts also announced the approach of the time during which Israel celebrated the great festivals of New Year, Tabernacles and the Day of Atonement.

Like the ram's horn at the beginning of Israel's New Year, the trumpets of chapters eight and nine certainly mark the approach of the great and final festival of God's triumph. The Chosen People have already been shown to be vested and in place before God's throne; they are ready to celebrate.

However, the trumpets of Revelation function even more strikingly as a call to repentance. Once we appreciate this aspect of the Seer's imagery then we also begin to see John's authentic concern for those afflicted by the plagues. The disasters are not just part of the plan God has for the good of his Chosen Ones; they are also meant to bring the people who suffer from them to salvation. Sadly, the Seer knows that even these desperate measures do not ensure that the opportunity is seized. In the tradition of many of Israel's ancient prophets, John tells us that many choose to reject the call to repentance, no matter what the cost to themselves might be.

Just like the story of the ten plagues in Exodus, these chapters of Revelation use images of mounting disaster to recount a story of God's mighty action on behalf of the Chosen People. The white-clad multitude stands resplendent in the midst of this section, for it is the story of their liberation. Even though they too suffer in their own way during the time of tribulation, they do so under divine protection. Even now they take part in the festival of triumph. John takes no delight in telling us tales of pointless anguish and destruction. The catastrophes the Seer relates are far from meaningless. They have an essential role in the unfolding of God's plan, for they sound like the trumpets of Israel's liturgy trying to call humanity back to God. That doesn't guarantee their success. After the sixth trumpet blast has sounded, Revelation 9:20-21 notes:

> The rest of humanity who had not been killed in these plagues had no change of heart about the works of their hands, to stop worshipping demons and idols of gold and silver and bronze and

stone and wood that can neither see nor hear nor walk around. Nor did they have any change of heart over their murders or their magical spells or their sexual filth or their thieveries.[4]

If John wants to describe real catastrophe for us, he does it in these verses. From John's viewpoint, the true disaster is the hardness of the human heart that produces oppression for God's People and stubbornly rejects any call to repentance.

Human Suffering and Models of God

When the Seer describes catastrophe, we can get the impression that he has let his imagination run away with him. The fearsome appearance of the four horsemen at the beginning of chapter six may be just about believable, but by the time we reach the description of horse-like locusts with human faces wearing crowns, clad with scales and armed with the stinging tails of scorpions, we have definitely reached into what we normally think of as the realm of fantasy.[5]

Yet, in his own way, John uses these images to come to terms with a side of reality that many of us ignore in our religious thinking – the fact that wars take place, famines rage, diseases run rampant and earthquakes wreak their havoc. Such things are not fanciful inventions of the type of minds that produce apocalypses; they are reported more often in news bulletins and newspapers than in the Book of Revelation. Many people find it extremely difficult to reconcile such things with the goodness of God. Instead they choose to see the cosmos as random, without God, and as ultimately meaningless.

Even though we ourselves might reject the agnostic or atheistic response that such people make, perhaps their stance is none other than a rejection of the faulty theology that often masquerades as faith. No honest person can deny the horrible presence of tragedies and disasters in the world; yet we seldom let this side of reality affect our picture of God and of the divine plan. Instead we mould

---

4. Something similar is related after the opening of the sixth seal in 6:16-17. People do not respond to the disasters by turning to God; they only make a vain attempt to hide from the divine wrath.

5. John is truly being imaginative in his description of the locusts but, as is his usual custom, he is building upon images already known to him. In the case of the locusts of 9:3-11, the Seer is thinking of the locusts of Joel 1:4-7 (and the horses of Joel 2:4-5).

a type of 'fair-weather' God who is responsible for all of the good things but who has no hand, act or part in anything negative. When we do this, we have chosen a demigod who can never be the biblical God of the world and all it contains; this kind of God is only fit for light work.

Tragedies of course are not only global; in fact they seem to bite hardest when they are private and personal. Our religious response to personal suffering is a fair indication of how well we have integrated life's negative side into our awareness of God and our faith. As we did when we considered different approaches to Jesus, we can construct a number of overlapping models of God's relationship to our personal disasters in order to help us find where our own attitudes lie.

The first model could be called 'God, the Problem-Solver'. God's function is very clear in this model: bad things just happen and, when they do, the Almighty's job is to answer my prayers, by a miracle if necessary. This model is right in affirming the authentic power of prayer, but unfortunately views this power with a certain tunnel vision. Those parts of the Good News that deal with suffering and the cross are left largely unheard and God's job is reduced to doing what we ask in prayer. Sometimes those who hold this model feel they have great belief in God, but that is not the same as having great faith. When a prayer that is very important to them goes unanswered, they are left in crisis. This model can show itself when patterns of prayer border on the superstitious, trying for the right formula or practice that will turn the secret lock and release the answer that they seek. Variations of this model have been called 'The Slot-Machine God' (if I put in the right prayers the answer should come out) and 'The God of the Bargains' ('I'll do this for you, Lord, if you do that for me'). Confidence in God is one thing, confidence that God will always do what I want is quite another.

The second model is at the other extreme and might be termed 'God, the Non-Interferer'. The world, especially the human world, runs by its own rules and God can't really be expected to get involved when bad things happen. Prayer has a function, but it is really that of helping me to centre myself and to be open to events and situations in a self-governing world. This model was very popular a generation ago with a certain brand of theology, and it holds an attraction for those for whom human freedom and dignity are central philosophical principles. But the deficiency of this model shows itself in its approach to prayer. As one theologian observed twenty years ago, if the most prayer can do is to reconcile me to the inevitable, a large brandy might work more quickly and effectively.

'God, the Cause of My Woes' is, surprisingly, a biblical model. We find it in such places as Psalm 88 where God is blamed for every woe that the author of the psalm experienced. It doesn't matter whether you call it punishing, rebuking or testing, many biblical texts speak of God causing suffering and hardship – sometimes, as in Jeremiah 20:7-18, even for those hardest at work in the divine service. This model is most strikingly expressed in the Book of Job. Job won't even agree that he is being punished or tested – God is just doing horrible things to Job at a whim. Few people today go to that extreme, but this way of thinking raises its head every time we cry to heaven, 'Why me?' (and few of us haven't made that cry at some time or other). This model has its obvious limitations, but at least it acknowledges honestly that our experience of the unpleasant and difficult side of life forms part of our experience of God.

Some people have a model of 'God Whose Will Is Always Done'. Every disaster, every catastrophe becomes the will of God without exception. The model has certainly avoided a simple optimism that insists that God always be 'nice', but at the cost of ultimately placing all blame for suffering on the Deity. This model is more often applied to someone else's tragedy rather than to my own and finds expression in the mouths of those attempting a quick and easy comforting of others at times of deep bereavement and loss. People who hold this model ignore the fact that there are many things taking place in the world that are quite obviously not the will of God, but the will of humanity. They fail to make a true distinction between good, which comes from God, and evil, which does not. The will of God cannot be used like a rubber stamp to sanction everything that happens or to label something evil as a divine act.

Which brings us to the final approach, 'God Who Is To Be Found in the Mystery of Suffering.' There are so many strands to this approach that it can hardly be termed a model at all. It doesn't attempt to explain where suffering comes from or why it is there. This approach only acknowledges that suffering is part of human experience. But this approach always insists that God is present in a person's suffering, not silent or absent as Job thought. The strands of this approach seem to trail off in various different directions: the acceptance of a cross, the response to lessen or remove the suffering of others, union with the suffering of Jesus, earnest prayer to the Lord who is close to the brokenhearted, or trust in the One who works all things to the good. Despite the variety of forms this approach takes in different people in different situations, it is held together by the trust that God has a loving plan which is not thwarted by this event or that misfortune. Everything that happens, no matter what the cause, provides an opportunity to seek – and to find – God within it.

The Seer's Picture of God and Suffering

The models outlined above apply to our ways of relating God to personal tragedy, not to the tragedies that make news headlines. Both the approach and the focus of the Seer are somewhat different. He has not written an essay that puts forth his views on individual suffering; his view is cosmic, and he writes his vision as a narrative using very broad strokes. Even so, John gives us a few points about the mysterious presence of evil and suffering in the world that are worth pondering both at individual and cosmic levels. We must note that the Seer makes no attempt to speak of everything bad that has ever happened to anyone. John would not necessarily apply what he has to say about the handful of events he relates to every earthquake, famine or flood that he knew of, and he certainly makes no claim to have ready answers to someone else's personal tragedy.

John's concern with the plan of God is evident throughout the Apocalypse, and this is his starting point as well when he narrates the plagues. While the Greek philosophers of this time posed questions about the existence and nature of the Deity – as we still tend to do when we get philosophical about religion – for Jews like John the real question was whether or not God ruled the world according to a plan and purpose. John's answer is a definite and resounding 'Yes', but with an equally clear acknowledgement that God's plan is not at work without interference. The clear connection found throughout the Scriptures between suffering and sin[6] always forms the backdrop to the plagues that John narrates; if there had been no sin in the world, these plagues would have no place in the unfolding of the divinely appointed course of events. The urgent necessity of God's plan demands that interference be overcome and removed; those who cause the interference bear the real responsibility for the presence of the horrors depicted in the Apocalypse.

John views these horrendous happenings as having a real part to play in God's plan – perhaps not in God's plan as it might unfold in a perfect world, but certainly in God's plan as it must take shape in a world deformed by sin. The plagues are not setbacks or lapses in God's care for the world but actually an aspect of the divine plan's progression. At the same time, the Seer does not give the impression that he views these disasters as anything other than something to be dreaded. John describes some of these arising from dark agents that are already present in the world, restrained until this time by the power of God. He uses language that implies that some of these forces are in rebellion against God, even though God now allows them to be unleashed so that they can play an unwitting part in the divine plan.[7] This could well be the Seer's way of expressing the distinction between God's causing evil to happen and God's turning of the evil that others cause to a divine purpose.[8]

---

6. In some parts of the Hebrew Bible, the connection between the evil of sin and the evil of suffering is made in nearly mathematical fashion: if you sin, you will suffer (in this life); if you are good, God will reward you (in this life). The Book of Job corrected this mechanical interpretation of God's dealings with individuals, but some people still seem to hold it. The New Testament also rejects the simple picture that only the guilty suffer and does so in many ways, not least by telling of how the sinless Servant of God suffered for us. At the same time, it makes clear that there is a deep (if not always traceable) connection between the presence of sin and the presence of suffering in the world. It may be that my sin makes you suffer, or that we both suffer because of the sin of someone we don't even know, but the connection is somehow there. In the biblical view, there is really no such thing as free-floating suffering that is not connected with someone's decision to act against God.

7. Notice the image of the fallen star in 9:1 (reminiscent of the language used of Satan in Luke 10:18), the fact that the plague of locusts operates under its own dark leader in 9:11 and the bondage of the murderous spirits in 9:13-15.

8. Classical Christian theology is very fond of this distinction and one might imagine that it belongs to the philosophies of the Middle Ages. In fact, its roots are to be found in the Hebrew Bible where evil chosen by human agents is turned to further the divine plan. However, the evil remains something undesired by God (as is evident from the fact that God will still punish it as evil); see, for instance, Jeremiah 25:3-13.

All forces get marshalled into the mighty march of the plan of God, even against their nature and will.

We must never imagine that the plan of God in the Apocalypse is some self-willed whimsy of an egocentric Deity. The plan is designed for the benefit of people, not just to the glory of God. Primarily the plan is there to bring about the liberation of the Chosen People shepherded by the Lamb in chapter seven. Even though the redeemed must also undergo suffering and tribulation, they are already in God's sheltering presence and their tears will be wiped away and forgotten. The full unfolding of the scroll, costly though it seems at times, will prove truly worthwhile for them. When this People is seen as the focus of the divine plan, then the plan's ultimate purpose of bringing relief, not causing suffering, comes through.

Yet those who are not part of the Chosen People are also embraced by the divine plan. Even though they may not respond, they are sent trumpet blasts earnestly calling them back to God. The workings of the plan do not shut out the idolater, the murderer, the occultist or the thief. The divine plan makes dramatic attempts to include them among those gathered before the throne of God, and these attempts can involve human suffering.

When we put these few points together, we see John's picture of a divine plan that includes human suffering because it must unfold in a sinful world. However, John shows us that the forces that cause suffering are already out there; now, as far as possible, these forces actually do something to further the plan of God. Even those who suffer from the disasters in John's visions have the chance for unimaginable gain, if only they respond to the plagues as God's call to repentance. The goal of the plan – the full salvation of God's redeemed – far excels in goodness the evil of the suffering that accompanies the plan's unfolding. The failure of this full salvation to materialise would be a far greater evil than all of the catastrophes and plagues in the Apocalypse rolled together.

Honestly Viewing the Reality of Evil

The Seer makes no claim to hand us ready answers to the problem of disaster and suffering, whether in world events or in our own lives. We would be abusing his book if we claimed to find such answers in these chapters. In any case, the apocalyptic form in which John expresses himself makes it likely that modern Western readers of Revelation will claim to find more problems than to find answers in any case.

John has managed to blend a strong and honest acknowledgement of tragedy and disaster in the world with his strong and honest faith. These dark realities, he insists, must be viewed within the context of a larger plan of God unfolding in the world, a plan that is totally concerned with redemption, liberation and salvation. Even the suffering is not totally negative; as a call to a radical change of heart, it can be an open door through which those now outside of God's redeemed can be counted among that number. And when the Chosen People themselves begin to tremble with dread at the horrors that happen in the world, John shows them a vision of themselves as already in the presence of God and under the shepherding protection of the Lamb. Once they recognise that God is at work on their behalf, they can celebrate already the salvation that God has begun to bring them.

John's outlook challenges our own tendency to view the unfolding of human history as if it were a process totally independent of the plan of God. The Seer does not pretend to give a divine motive and objective for each event even in the context of a vision. John gives us no licence to claim that, when a particular event occurred, God had such-and-such in mind. No, the Seer only wants us to see that a divine plan is at work in the unfolding of the world's story, even at those times when God seems most absent. He also demands that we drop the deceptive notion that, in our sinful reality, there could have been a different divine plan in which tragedy and suffering had no place. That wasn't the case at the Exodus; that wasn't the case at Calvary; and it can't be the case now.

By setting his plagues against the background of the divine plan and by revealing to us his glorious vision of the People for whom that plan is formed, John cautions us against viewing tragic events solely in a negative light. What can truly be termed disastrous when viewed in isolation can be seen more positively in light of the full picture. The Seer speaks primarily to communities of disciples about the suffering, dread and fear they face in the time of tribulation. He is certainly not throwing around platitudes to individuals suffering personal tragedies and losses. John shows us both sides of the picture: the authenticity of horror and suffering, but also the reality of something that is beyond suffering and in which we participate even now through faith. Once again, John will not permit us to finish thinking about any event without acknowledging that God is at work, even if we cannot begin to trace the precise lines of the divine presence and involvement.

Finally, Revelation invites us to hear once more the call to repentance that is sometimes contained in the mystery of human suffering. Christians today have been discouraged from listening for this call by the eagerness of some to point self-righteous fingers and to dress themselves up as heralds of divine wrath. That is hardly what John would have us do. Throughout the New Testament, repentance means having a change of heart, discovering what is wrong and choosing what is right instead. Disasters and suffering can act as trumpet calls to repentance by pointing to something wrong with the way we have chosen to live, beckoning us to healing and forgiveness. The Seer does not paint them as heavenly lightning bolts making direct hits on the guilty. Remember, in John's vision the plagues spare many who are as sinful as the ones who were afflicted. If he had intended to show the Almighty engaging in an act of strict retribution, the Seer should have told us of an even higher body-count.

In recent decades, some religious people have made a false interpretation of the disastrous outbreak of sexually transmitted diseases in general and AIDS in particular. They claim that this is a divine judgment on drug abusers and those engaged in homosexual acts. This approach ignores the many people who have contracted these diseases in other ways, and at times gives the impression of shedding few tears for the victims of these afflictions. If such people were right, those who try to work for a cure for AIDS could be accused of trying to interfere with the plan of God. Such thinking is far removed from the type of picture John presents to us. However, if these diseases helped us to suspect that something is radically wrong with our sexual attitudes and behaviour, if we heard the trumpet urging us to think out our values again, then we would be making an interpretation of events that the Seer might recognise.

Breaking Seals and Blaring Trumpets (Rev 6:1-9:21)

Since the spread of AIDS is so closely related to an explicitly moral issue, it could be a poor example to take. The suffering that occurs in various forms in the Third World might prove a better one. We who live in more stable and affluent societies often think of the poverty of the Third World in terms of natural causes mixed in with a certain amount of luck. Seldom do we reflect on the past and present exploitation of the Third World by developed nations as undermining the infrastructures of Third World societies and depriving them of their resources. If we began to look at ourselves and our lifestyles as being part of the cause of the Third World poverty that we superficially regret, then we would be hearing the trumpet call to repentance that sounds in this human suffering. Instead, we demand cheap coffee, cheap oil and the products of cheap labour as if these things could come without costing anyone a penny – and deafen ourselves even to trumpet blasts.

The mystery of suffering is deeper than the ocean and darker than the night. The Seer's approach was never intended to pierce all the clouds in which suffering is wrapped. Some people will find other biblical approaches to be more attractive and more helpful to their particular situations. They might be inspired by Hosea's struggle with his own personal tragedy; only his broken heart could discover a new dimension to the relationship between God and Israel that brought healing to his own suffering. From others, like the figure of Jonah, we can learn something of how suffering holds the key to finding the love of God and to understanding some of God's seemingly senseless actions. Many Christians have found strength in the approach to suffering contained in that great treatise on Jesus' sacrifice, the Letter to the Hebrews. Those who are in the midst of their own trials can find an inspiring spirituality of suffering in passages from Philippians and Colossians; anyone undergoing his or her private tribulations will recognise there the message of faith uttered by the voice of experience. The Word of God gives us a variety of approaches to suffering, yet never, never attempts to dispel the mystery itself.

However, we would be depriving ourselves greatly if we took the variety offered in the Scriptures as a licence to set the Seer's approach to one side. John has an important place in the vast biblical mosaic depicting suffering and the presence of evil in the world. He has earned it by daring to take what is most dreadful, what is most repugnant and what is most horrendous and insisting that, even in these things, we can find God and celebrate with joy. If we make our own faltering steps down the path John wishes to lead us, then we might discover with him the God who is truly Lord of the earth and all it contains. And if we don't? Well, we might be stuck with a rather fragile God who has to be kept under wraps on stormy days.

Questions for Reflection and Prayer

1. How can the plagues of Revelation 6-9 contain Good News? Would we do well to skip this section of Revelation because of the destruction it recounts in horrific detail?

2. Our religious response to personal suffering is an indication of how we integrate life's negative side into our awareness of God and our faith. Which model of God is most typical of how you react to personal suffering or tragedy?

3. The Seer views the horrendous things he describes as having a real part to play in God's plan, for the goal of that plan far exceeds in goodness the evil of suffering that accompanies its unfolding. Can the Seer's perspective be of encouragement to those undergoing their own personal tragedy?

4. The Seer's approach to the mystery of suffering was never intended to pierce all the clouds in which it is wrapped. Which biblical approach to the mystery of suffering do you find most helpful?

5

Three and a Half Years

Revelation 10:1 – 11:18

On more than one occasion my spiritual director has reminded me that all divine attributes are without limit. Therefore, he claims, God has an infinite sense of humour.

One doesn't need to be a great theologian to notice this. For instance, God has given me the gift of being a reasonably punctual person. Then the divine sense of humour comes into play, for I am also given the gift of close friends who are anything but punctual. One was once twenty-four hours late in picking me up at the airport (not that I waited for him). Sometimes one can laugh, listening to the improbable excuses for the delays and disappointments; but then there are other times when even an infinite and divine sense of humour fails to raise a smile.

Long-suffering has brought its own kind of wisdom. For instance, I now know that, while there is no end to the variety of unpunctualities and excuses, there are just two basic types of waiting. The first type is predominated by the deceptive feeling that arrival is imminent, so it's not worth trying to do anything in the meantime except wait. This produces paralysis; all concentration is given to the very act of waiting while reciting the mantra 'They're bound to show up at any minute now.' The second type takes the period of waiting as an unscheduled opportunity to get things done. According to the first type, the period of waiting is time stolen from one's day; in the second type, the period of waiting gives you a gift of time that you wouldn't otherwise have had.

The Second Coming of Jesus has always posed the problem of waiting for disciples. Despite the fact that we have been told that a lot needs to be done in preparation for the Second Coming, from the very beginning some Christians have decided that the world's sure passing is a good excuse for doing nothing. According to one interpretation of 2 Thessalonians 3:6-13, Paul had to deal with a few members of the Thessalonian Church who decided that they no longer had to work for a living now that the world was coming to an end. Reading the New Testament itself on the coming of the

Kingdom should plant a very different idea in our minds: there is so much to be done that idleness is not an option.

In the Meantime

Since Revelation speaks of the long awaited dawning of God's Kingdom, we might expect it to give some indication of what disciples are meant to do in the meantime before the coming of the Kingdom.

Even the idea of the 'meantime' has always posed its own problems in Christian thought. In the earliest days of the Church some seemed to believe that this period would be so short that they couldn't be expected to do much of anything with it apart from announcing the Kingdom. Most of the New Testament writings certainly reflect a belief that the Second Coming can happen at any time, but not necessarily as soon as we might expect it. The New Testament leaves us in no doubt that the period between the death and resurrection of Jesus and his Second Coming – however long or short it might prove to be – was meant to be productive. But the strange approaches to the timing of this intervening period continue. There are still groups who confidently predict the return of Jesus at a specific time, despite the type of warnings given in Matthew 24:36-42. Equally lamentable is the tendency of other Christians to deny that the world is in a 'meantime'. Whether in theory or in practice, they forget about the Second Coming altogether or equate it with the moment of personal demise. If we are to evaluate and use the meantime correctly, we need a stronger belief in the coming of the Kingdom than that.

John not only shows us a period before the Second Coming; he actually measures it. The span he assigns to it is three years and a half year (or 1,260 days), another symbolic number. This use of symbolism indicates that John hasn't made the mistake of trying to figure out the day and the hour. We have already seen that seven generally stands for completeness and fullness, so that this half-seven signals something incomplete and partial. The symbolism runs even deeper, for John takes the figure from the length of time in the Book of Daniel[1] during which Israel will suffer and the

---

1. The actual phrase used by Daniel is 'for a time and times and half a time'; see Daniel 7:25 and 12:7. Revelation uses this same phrase in 12:14.

powers of evil will dominate just before the manifestation of God's Kingdom. The Seer tells us by this number that there is a length of time which, though long enough, is limited in the divine plan. Suffering and evil will be strongly present for this period, but will end in the final coming of the Kingdom. When he describes a few scenes as lasting three and a half years, John does not braid a string of such periods, but makes us look from different viewing points at this one penultimate period leading to the manifestation of the Kingdom.

The Role of the Seer

Before John even mentions the three and a half years, he tells us something about his own task. From the very beginning of his vision into the heavenly Sanctuary, the Seer must have suspected that he would be given a job to do. After all, jobs often went with visions. When Isaiah saw the glory of God in the Temple and when Ezekiel saw that same glory in exile, both prophets were commissioned to go and deliver God's message to Israel. The very same thing happens to the Seer in chapter ten. He inherits Isaiah's and Ezekiel's mantle and is told that he too must prophesy.

In this passage, three aspects of the Seer's prophesying role come to the fore. We have just witnessed through John's eyes the unsealing of the great scroll of God's plan and might well expect to learn of its contents. We don't. Instead John is given a 'little scroll'. This indicates that John's prophesy is a limited one; even though John's little scroll deals with matters that the great scroll is also concerned with, there is much it does not contain. It is a scroll written for John and his audience, especially concerned with the present and future as it affects them, a scroll for the 'meantime' before the Kingdom is fully revealed.[2] A different audience would have been given a different scroll.

The second thing John tells us is that he is not even free to communicate everything that he has seen and heard. He hears the voice of seven thunders (which we can surmise signal a message no

---

2. The angel's posture in Revelation 10:5-7, touching as it does the three zones of heaven, land and sea, indicates the cosmic significance of what is on the little scroll even though its contents are limited. The giving of the little scroll is a dramatic reminder that the God of the Cosmos has made a very special place in the great plan even for John's churches, and for our own as well.

less dramatic than that of the seven seals and seven trumpets) but John is forbidden to reveal what he heard in those seven thunders. Once more the Seer points to the limitations of his task and of the message he bears.

John communicates a third point when he speaks of eating the scroll. The same symbolic action was demanded of Ezekiel (in Ezekiel 2:9-3:3) to teach him that a prophet must be nourished and filled with the Word of God. The sweetness of John's scroll indicates that it is Good News, and this image too is drawn from Ezekiel. But the Seer has an experience that Ezekiel did not have: the scroll turns bitter in the stomach. Good News though it may be, the scroll also contains sorrow and bitterness, especially as it deals with 'many peoples and nations and tongues and kings' (10:11). Any mental image that one may have constructed of John as one who relishes the disasters he foretells for non-Christians must be abandoned here. The Seer knows that the total picture is Good News and rejoices in it; but he is deeply troubled by the suffering and afflictions that must accompany the unfolding of God's plan.

Pictures of the Meantime Church

When the Seer is told as part of his prophetic commissioning to measure the Sanctuary and its altar, he brings the last chapters of the Book of Ezekiel very much to mind. Beginning with chapter 40, Ezekiel tells how he was shown a vision of a new temple for God's glory and that he measured it and all of its features with painstaking care. One scholar, speaking of these chapters of Ezekiel, remarked that, when most prophets are given a vision, they tremble or fall on their faces, yet here is Ezekiel casually reaching for his measuring tape and notebook. Of course, there is more to Ezekiel's action than that. The act of measuring stakes a claim. It is a declaration that what is measured shall not be diminished. It shows protective, watchful and even jealous ownership.

The sanctuary and altar John measures are obviously not the heavenly Sanctuary into which John has been permitted to gaze, but some sort of earthly sanctuary. Like the Jerusalem Temple, there is a whole complex of structures and courts attached to the Seer's temple that indicate different levels of holiness. The measuring applies to the inmost realities alone, and only these are protected. The rest falls to whoever happens to take it over.

When he wrote about the Gentiles[3] trampling the outer courts of the Temple, John could well have in mind the destruction of the Jerusalem Temple in 70 AD, an event that grieved Jewish Christians like John very deeply indeed. Although he too mourns the loss of that outward Temple, John knows that the inner reality, of which any earthly temple could be but a symbol, will continue untouched and undamaged.

Even if this passage reflects the Roman destruction of the Jerusalem edifice, it affirms above all the protection of the Temple that is God's People. The act of measuring protects an innermost reality that remains most jealously guarded, but it also warns that there is an aspect of God's People that will be trampled and fall under the power of others. The Seer perhaps intended us to think of the Israelites who did not become disciples or of the disciples who fall away as constituting the outer courts, but certainly he also wanted us to recognise in them the powerless suffering that the Church was called to endure for three and a half years.

The first picture we are given of these three and a half years, then, has a double edge. As Church, we are to be the protected ones worshipping before God's throne. But we are also to be the suffering, powerless ones, trampled at the whim of the nations as if there were nothing sacred or divine about us at all. But only for three and a half years.

No sooner is the Temple measured than we are given another picture of the Church in this 'meantime' drawn with images from Israel's prophets. Zechariah 4:1-14 relates a vision of a golden lampstand (a sign of the presence of God in the Sanctuary) and two olive trees. The two trees that feed the lampstand are identified as the high priest and the prince of the House of David, the two Anointed Ones of God who worked for the restoration of the Temple and its services after its destruction in the sixth century BC.

---

3. The term 'Gentile' applies to any non-Jew. Translations of the Bible use a variety of words for Gentiles, including 'nations' and 'pagans'. The New Testament use varies according to the situation in which the term is used. It can mean all those who are not part of the Chosen People (whether we make that term mean primarily Israel or Church), those of pagan stock within the Church, or nations in a political sense. The terms 'Gentile' and 'nations' often carry a negative overtone except when they are applied to non-Jewish Christians.

In the Seer's application of this image to the Church, the two figures are both lampstands and olive trees; in other words, they are simultaneously testifying to the presence of God and putting themselves at the active service of that presence. It is also significant that there are two of them, for in Israel's Law witnesses were always to be two in number. It seems that, no matter how many witnesses there were to an incident, they were heard only in pairs. According to 11:6-7, the chief task of these figures in Revelation is to bear testimony through prophecy. What the Seer has been called to do within the Church, the Church is called to do in the great city of the human world.[4]

The picture of the prophesying mission of the Church teems with power. It reflects the status of Zechariah's two lampstands who are nothing less than the Anointed of God. So too, says John, the Church is the Anointed of God with all of the dignity, responsibility and power that goes with that status. Ancient Israel's respect for prophets as bearers of God's Word led them to think of the prophets of the past as powerful figures. Whatever prophets said happened; whatever they prayed for, they got. John, by saying that these two witnesses have available to them the powers of fire, drought and plague, does not mean to represent them as destructive or vindictive, but as people who carry the powerful authority of the Word of God. This authority also protects them and ensures that their testimony is fully given, but there is no total protection of their persons. They are killed. The people of the city rejoice because they think that the witnesses are vanquished. If the period of their testimony is limited (three and a half years), then their apparent vanquishing lasts only for a period that is so limited that it is nearly insignificant – three and a half days.

---

4. Sometimes more specific identification of these figures and the great city of 11:8 is suggested. In the early Church, the two witnesses were occasionally seen as Old Testament figures (Moses and Elijah or Elijah and Elisha); and some have proposed that they stand for Peter and Paul or the sons of Zebedee. Similarly interpreters sometimes suggest that the great city is a code for either Rome or Jerusalem. The Seer may well be drawing from specific individuals or cities when he writes this passage (or others), but he is not drawing portraits of historical individuals for us to identify. The weighty amount of symbolic detail included in this scene tells us that John is sketching on a broader canvas; he is trying to show something of the relationship between the Church and the world in which it must operate. The resulting picture applies in some way to figures that embody in their individual lives what John shows of the life of the Church.

The Church in the Great City

Some of John's churches, as we have seen, were situated in great and important cities like Ephesus and Pergamum. As a religious grouping, Christians must have felt very small compared to the magnificent evidence of pagan worship all around them: the impressive temples, the powerful priesthoods, the pageants and festivals, the public sacrifices – worship which reflected the might and glory of the Roman empire itself. Most of the other people living in these cities would not have known much about Christianity, if they had heard of it at all. Many pagans would have lumped Christians together with Jews as different branches of the same strange religion. Since Judaism itself was often despised, this wasn't exactly good publicity for disciples. To be a Christian in Asia Minor at the end of the first century must have been very discouraging.

When John shows his churches a picture of themselves in the midst of their cities and their world in Revelation 11, he captures some of this feeling. The witnesses are greatly outnumbered (a whole city's population to two), despised and eventually killed. Yet, for all that, they have a job to do and they are given the power to do it. We should also note that, despite the picture of utter rejection and failure contained in this scene, we are clearly told in 11:13 that *something* worked – in the end, a great part of the city finally gave glory to God.

The Church and civil society have interacted in many different ways over two thousand years of the Church's history. The New Testament writings, composed as they were in situations when few influential figures were Christian, contain a surprising number of admonitions to obey the state and to honour those in positions of power. Acts of the Apostles, especially in some of the speeches of St Paul, shows a concern to have the civil powers recognise that Christianity is a respectable religion and worthy of society's tolerance. This effort to demonstrate the civil respectability of Christianity continued for the first few centuries, and occasionally the effort was directed in writing to the person of the reigning emperor. This contact between Church and the powers of the state shows no real effort on the part of Christianity to control civil society. With the freedom of the Church under Constantine, things began to change markedly. As Christianity acted more and more as a state religion, the Church found itself increasingly in the position of moulding society and influencing its structures. This was particularly true of the interplay that took place between Christian values and civil law.

Today in the Western world, the Church is left with a very mixed heritage. On the one hand, as Church we have inherited the vestiges of influence and even power in secular society and naturally feel the obligation to use this influence responsibly. On the other, the Church no longer lives in a society which can be presumed to be Christian, even theoretically. While Christians may form the vast majority of the population, members of other faiths and those of no faith are as fully members of a state as its Christian citizens are. The thorny problem soon shows itself: to what extent should Christian values which are rejected by other citizens of a state influence the laws and society of the state itself? What responsibility does the Church now have for forming the civil society around it?

One group would feel that Christians continue to bear a responsibility for influencing society that was appropriate to popes and bishops of mediaeval Christendom. The Church, they would argue, should use every means at its disposal to ensure that Christian values are the sure foundation for the laws of the land. A similar ideal – expressed very differently – is put forward by a second group who feel that one of the central tasks of the Church is to build a just society, although the actual result they have in mind might differ radically from what many in the first group would demand of a Christian society. The first group can contain some very conservative outlooks, the second some very liberal ones.

A different approach insists on a sharp demarcation between religious belief of any kind, Christianity included, and political realities. The phrase 'separation of Church and State' is often used in this context. Such an approach in its extreme form would argue that individual citizens should refrain from bringing any value held on religious grounds into the public arena. This position is held by many who claim no religious conviction, but it is also held by many Christians who look upon religion as being essentially a private matter. Political figures who are Christians sometimes plead that there is no other workable approach.

The mixture of outlooks results in very basic differences of strategy and emphasis among those who hold identical values. The unfortunate result is that burning topics which touch on central Christian values kindle conflict, suspicion and accusation within the Christian community itself. I may conclude that the local grocer is not as committed to the value of life as I am because she will not put up a poster publicising my anti-abortion rally. I may feel that the shopper who does not boycott the products of that multinational as a protest against its Third World exploitation (as I do) is not really as committed to justice as I am. Because I have jumped to the illogical conclusion that those who agree with my values will naturally agree with my strategies and short-term goals, I find myself condemning those who truly treasure the same ideals instead of working with them and learning from them.

Beside this problem of strategy, the difference of opinion about how closely Christian values can be brought to bear on specific circumstances also produces quandaries of its own. After many a sermon touching on contemporary issues, a rebuke 'to stick to religion' is given to the bemused priest who is convinced that he had done exactly that.

The question of the influence of the Church in civil society has become so tangled that it will continue to cause new problems in every new situation to which it relates. However, the best approach to a tangle is to identify the beginning of a string or two and to work from there.

Since the New Testament was not written at a time when Christianity could be a major force in enshrining its values in society, it gives little guidance on some of the questions that we would most like to ask. The Seer, for instance, does not suggest what laws should be passed by the Roman Senate to counteract the many evils that existed in the society of his day – no more than Jesus expended great energy on structural social reform in his own ministry. Both Jesus and the Seer felt free to identify what was wrong with the societies in which they worked, even to name names; but if we look for their suggestions about what political action should be taken to correct these things and so to better society, we search in vain.

To help us attack the tangle, the Seer addresses a far more basic question than the one of Church influence on civil society and its laws. In Revelation 11:4-12, he identifies the basic relationship of the Church to wider human society as one of witness. In doing so John brings together a theme that is to be found in many forms in various parts of the New Testament. By linking the Church's vocation of witness to the task of the Israelite prophets, John also shows that the testimony of the Church will be largely unpopular, a thorn in the side to many who hear it.

John's insight is a liberating one. While there is a great responsibility to give testimony clearly and insistently, the Seer's vision frees the community of faith from all responsibility for the testimony's acceptance. We are freed from taking the blame for society's rejection of this or that value – as long as we have given our witness to the truth as well as we can. We may lament when our civil structures encourage depravity or our laws make legal that which we know to go against the most basic laws of God; but we must also be comforted that such developments do not signal any failure in our discipleship or any setback in God's plan to bring the Kingdom. John's insistence that the job of the Church is to bear witness, even unsuccessfully, should put political achievement very far down the Church's list of priorities. When political success for Christian values rises as a priority, there is a danger that the prophesying and witnessing aspects of the Church's vocation have been exchanged for a parody of what our true task should be.

Perhaps the history of the Church's efforts to implement aspects of Christianity through political efforts provides the clearest indication that we *can* step outside the terms of our mission. Certainly, there have been worthwhile achievements in this area that anyone can applaud, such as the cessation of gladiatorial combat in the Roman Empire or the ending of the slave trade. But then there were also the Crusades that, in using the wrong means to defend Christianity, produced so many things contrary to gospel values. There were abominable state laws in different places that required people to worship as members of the state Church. The fiasco of Prohibition in America was, at least, in part produced by churches attempting to address a social evil by converting their values into political results. One gets the feeling that, when churches turn to politics, the Spirit does not always succeed in filling them with wisdom and counsel. Once we stray from our mission, we can find ourselves making messes, even if they are the results of very fine intentions indeed.

I have been careful to speak of the Church (and the churches) in making these tentative applications of the Seer's picture. The picture changes somewhat when we think of individual disciples and their role in society. When the Church acts politically, it acts on a presumption that there is but one valid Christian approach to a burning topic, at times enshrining it in a single goal or a single strategy. When we remember that individual disciples find themselves with a variety of gifts and opportunities, the possibilities increase for the ways in which Christian values can influence society. These individual efforts become integrated into the wider task of the Church's witness without exchanging the God-given task of prophecy for more transient goals of social change. Although some individuals may devote themselves with great energy and generosity to a particular issue, the Church cannot afford to distort the gospel by focusing solely on those values that are under threat at a given time. Any Christian value taken out of the context of the full message of God's love becomes distorted, sometimes even dangerous. There is no such thing as a single-issue gospel. If we as Church find ourselves giving the impression that we are obsessed with one or two values, then we are no longer truly witnessing and prophesying according to our call.

Christianity is political by its very nature and necessarily makes its impact upon the societies in which disciples live and work. Like John the Seer before us, we continue to agonise over society's ills. Individual Christians cannot but respond in a variety of ways to those who fall victim to social evil. Such responses need a sense of urgency fired by the very love of God living within us. Yet, as Church, the primary task given to us always remains to act the prophet and to bear testimony to the Good News to the great city that does not accept it.

Concern with specific practical political results must take second place to this God-given mission. Political concerns can subvert and distort the Church's mission, no matter how noble the feelings and commitment behind them. Neither the churches nor individual disciples can substitute working for a better human society, governed by just laws and structures, for the goal of the Kingdom that demands nothing less than the inner conversion of human hearts.

The Heavenly Liturgy Concludes

John has shown us so many scenes since the end of chapter five that we might have well forgotten that we are still in the midst of a heavenly liturgy. The sounding of the final trumpet in 11:15-18 brings that liturgy to its conclusion with a crescendo. The Kingdom has come, we hear, and the joyful worship of the elders brings the ceremony to an end. Yet we who are told of this scene are more tantalised than satisfied. We are not shown the Kingdom, nor are we given any of the details of God's final triumph.

The Seer is bringing the first half of his book to an end together with the liturgy. He has now finished giving us the overview of God's great plan and shown his churches in broad terms how they fit into that plan. He has indicated that the sacrifice of the Lamb has entered the heavenly Sanctuary and its effects in history will result in times of tribulation, tasks to be done and the sure triumph of God's Kingdom.

But John still has much to say about the 'meantime' Church. He is still free to report scenes from the heavenly Sanctuary that help us to understand the workings of the divine plan, but his gaze turns much more towards the human world now. The Seer knows that we need help in interpreting these three and a half years and what they contain. There are so many possibilities for confusion, so many forces going about in fancy dress that John now sets himself to the task of lifting masks and stripping off disguises. The spiritual adventure is about to enter an even more challenging phase for those of us who wait.

Questions for Reflection and Prayer

1. Christians through the ages have understood the period of waiting for the Second Coming in different ways. The Seer speaks of a symbolic period of 'three years and a half year'. What is your personal response to the 'meantime' waiting period?

2. The Church in the Western world has been left with a very mixed

Three and a Half Years (Rev 10:1–11:18)

heritage through the interaction between Christian values and civil law and society. What role does the Church have today in influencing or forming the civil society around it?

3. By linking the Church's vocation of witness to the task of the Israelite prophets, John's vision highlights the believing community's responsibility to bear witness clearly and insistently, while freeing it from all responsibility for the testimony's acceptance. What are the implications of this liberating insight for Christians today?

4. Since Christianity is political by its very nature and impacts on societies in which disciples live and work, in what way can the Seer's approach give renewed focus and perspective to Christians in 'the great city'?

6
The Great Sign

Revelation 11:19 – 12:18

While ignorance has many drawbacks that anyone can see, occasionally it has its advantages: it can allow us to undertake commitments and projects that we would otherwise avoid. We have all had our 'if only I knew then what I know now' experiences.

I had one such experience years ago when, as a young curate, I volunteered to bring the altar-servers to a film in town and then to a fast-food restaurant where I had arranged refreshments. During the days coming up to the event, I shrugged off the occasional compliment to my bravery in this undertaking. 'Of course I'll be able to manage on my own. Sure, there are just thirty-five of them and I'll only have them for a couple of hours.'

On the day, I found that getting them to stay still long enough to have a headcount and manage them into the cinema auditorium was a difficult achievement and persuading them to sit together a major triumph. During the show itself, although I was very vigilant, I saw little of the film. Afterwards, the boys (servers were all male in those days) tried to entertain me with stories of how other members of the group had misbehaved during the film, but unfortunately I was not quite in the mood to enjoy these tales as they thought. That day I also learned that any given group of thirty-five altar-servers needs thirty-five special orders. Altogether, it was an experience.

The film we saw was *Raiders of the Lost Ark* and, at a very long stretch, one could say that it might have brought the biblical Ark of the Covenant to their attention (though not in a way that anyone concerned with their religious education would think useful). But they did enjoy it, they were grateful, and it was an adventure.

The Seer's Adventure
As we enter the second major part of John's book, we have more than tasted the Seer's spiritual adventure. We have seen sights that are normally hidden from our eyes. Once John has pointed out to us some of the wonders in his vision, we might find ourselves noticing them a bit more, even when we aren't thinking about his

The Great Sign (Rev 11:19–12:18)

book: the unique place of Christ, the earthly and heavenly reality of the Church, the centrality of the Lamb's sacrifice, the mysterious working out of the divine plan.

Yet it still might not have struck us to ask for whom the Seer's spiritual adventure was intended. The word 'spiritual' could have made us answer that question prematurely, for it often evokes thoughts of one's private relationship to the Transcendental. Spiritual reading and spiritual exercises are traditionally matters done with a certain degree of isolation from others, and conversations with a spiritual director are conducted in the utmost privacy. Since spirituality also embraces a level of self-knowledge, spirituality gets confused with introspection and even with pop-psychology. You could be forgiven for thinking that spirituality's major focus is the individual side of religion.

But the Seer has not invited us as individuals into his spiritual adventure. He makes it clear from the start that he is speaking to churches. Adventures, even spiritual ones, are like birthday parties — they are hard to have on your own. Of course John is appealing to the individuals who make up these communities, but what he is revealing affects them first and foremost as communities. As he presents his message, the Seer is also revealing his own multifaceted spirituality. By this stage it becomes more and more evident that John's spirituality is not self-centred but Church-centred. John is keenly aware of his own special calling and relationship to God, that God has called him by name, but it is all in the context of the Church with its multitudinous members, each of whom God has also called by name. In this Church-centredness John is at one with the greatest spiritual writers and mystics of Christian tradition, notwithstanding the individual emphasis that sometimes is given to our ordinary use of the word 'spiritual'.

All spiritual theology recognises the need for self-knowledge as a basis for developing an authentic relationship with God. We as Church need this self-knowledge just as individuals do. That is why the Seer has a vision of Church running so prominently through his book. At the very beginning of the spiritual adventure, John's churches saw themselves honoured to be lampstands signalling the presence of God in the heavenly Sanctuary. The picture communicated something of their oneness before God, even though these churches were also scattered into different cities and communities on the earth. The churches of Asia Minor were also told in blunt terms that they could be flickering and spluttering, in need of trimming by the High Priest before the celestial liturgy could go any further. They were shown their true place at the centre of the divine plan and given a preview of the numberless multitude that the Church is destined to become. The portrait of Church in the first eleven chapters was noble, dignified, glorious, but not without its brush strokes of challenge, tribulation and work to be done.

Now that the Seer begins a new part of his book, he presents us with a new picture of Church. The first part of the Apocalypse unfolded the larger scroll of the great plan of God. Now the Seer calls the attention of his communities to more immediate matters that belong more to the little scroll entrusted to him. John is ready to unveil more about this time of three and a half years in which his seven churches of Asia Minor find themselves. In order to enter this phase of the spiritual adventure, the seven churches need an even clearer awareness of what they are as Church, and John begins to lead them into this with the monumental scenes he depicts in chapter twelve.

The Ark Appears in Heaven

> And the Temple of God that is in heaven was opened and his Ark of the Covenant was revealed in his Sanctuary. And there were lightning flashes and soundings and thunderings and an earthquake and heavy hail. (Rev 11:19)

I wonder if any of the altar-servers who watched *Raiders of the Lost Ark* with me would find it helpful in understanding this text. He would probably ask where the Nazis and the floppy-hatted archaeologist had got to. All the same, that film fantasy and the Apocalypse agree on at least two points about the Ark: first, the Ark of the Covenant was held to be a potent instrument of God's might in battle; second, the whereabouts of the Ark is no longer known to humankind. It is also possible that popular tales and belief that the Ark's reappearance will herald supernatural victories have influenced both the film's script-writers and the Seer, albeit in different ways.

The Great Sign (Rev 11:19–12:18)

With all due respect to the script-writers, the Seer's knowledge and appreciation of the traditions surrounding the Ark far outstripped anything my altar-servers could possibly have gleaned from their film. John knew of the Ark as the supreme symbol of the presence of Yahweh with Israel, leading them with power into the Promised Land and enshrined among them in the Jerusalem Temple. The Ark may have been designed for carrying with its handles and poles, but its final resting in the Temple stood as proof that God had chosen Israel, the House of David, and Jerusalem's holy mountain on which the Temple stood.

The holy mountain in Jerusalem was known in biblical times as Mount Zion.[1] For ancient Israel, it was far more than a simple geographical location, far more sacred for the people than any place on earth is for Christians today. Since it was the site of Yahweh's permanent resting among the Chosen People, speaking of Zion became a powerful way in which to speak of Israel's unique relationship to God. The fact that Zion housed both the royal palace and the Temple built by David's house associated this holy mountain with God's two great promises to David: that God would dwell in the Temple and that a son of David would always be king. Even though Zion usually refers to the holy mountain, the term also applies to the city of Jerusalem and sometimes was used for the whole nation that gathered on Zion to worship. All of these traditions are sometimes bundled together under the single figure of Daughter Zion, a woman who enjoys a special, tender relationship to Yahweh.

When the Seer tells us of the Ark reappearing in heaven (after an absence that lasted for over half a millennium), we know that the might of God is about to be unleashed with unbelievable force. Now, John tells us, God is really about to get to work. But the reappearance of the Ark should also remind us of the power and reliability of God's ancient promises: the Chosen People will always be under God's special care; God will always remain with them; and a son of David will rule them forever.

---

1. Sometimes spelled as 'Sion'. In later times, due to a misreading of certain biblical texts, another mountain in Jerusalem became identified as Mount Zion while the Temple Mount was referred to as Mount Moriah. Pilgrims to Jerusalem today are given these later identifications.

A Woman Clothed with the Sun

As impressed as we should be with John's vision of the Ark, he wants us to be more impressed by the Woman Clothed with the Sun. This, he tells us, is a great sign.[2] Since she appears garbed with various heavenly lights, she is meant to be dazzling in her splendour. Scholars often point out how the Seer has pulled out all the stops to tell us about the Woman and her story. A close study of chapter twelve and its background shows that John has not only taken language from Israel's Scriptures, he has also borrowed from various traditions popular in Judaism at his time and even from the pagan myths and ceremonies his churches would have known, living as they did in the midst of pagan cities. John wanted to decorate this great sign with anything that came to hand.

But who is the Woman? She is given a solid description, but enters the vision unnamed; in this, her appearance in John's narrative is not unlike that of the Lamb in chapter five. A pagan reader of the Apocalypse would probably have mistaken the Woman for a goddess – maybe even for the popular goddess Isis, who was often dressed in celestial garb, or for Ephesus's moon-goddess Artemis. Christian readers, however, would have known the true identity of this figure: the Woman is the Church, the People of God.[3]

John's great sign shows that the Church is more than just the collection of people who believe in Jesus. He shows us the Church as Daughter Zion, beloved of God and bearer of all the hopes and

---

2. The term 'sign' (sometimes translated as 'portent') has great force in the New Testament. It is often the preferred word to describe the miracles of Jesus and it can carry the sense of 'wonder'. If the Seer had only described the Woman as a sign, it would be noteworthy enough. His description of her as 'a great sign' means that her appearance should overwhelm us as well as make us determined to discover what God is revealing to us through this sign.

3. From the evidence that has survived, the identification of the Woman with the Church seems to have been the only one known in the early Church. A further identification of the Woman as Mary, the Mother of the Lord, will be familiar to many readers, but this interpretation of the Woman (which seems to depend mainly upon the Woman's act of giving birth in 12:5) was a much later suggestion. Even commentators on the passage who agree with a Marian identification are careful to note that this is not the first thing in the Seer's mind. If Mary is to be seen in this passage, it is only through the lens of Mary as image and mother of the Church. The tendency to read Revelation 12 in light of Marian devotion has enriched the way that Mary is depicted in Christian art by applying some of the symbolic imagery of this chapter to her in traditional iconography.

The Great Sign *(Rev 11:19–12:18)*

promises that God ever gave to humanity. As he paints this portrait, the Seer's brush dabs deftly into the many bold and pastel colours that he has mixed from the Hebrew Bible. She shines like the sun and moon, an amazing show of mighty splendour (Song 6:10), adorned with the dazzling figures of Israel's past such as Jacob, Rachel and the ancestors of the twelve tribes (Gen 37:9-10). She goes forth to give birth, mother of the child of promise and indeed of the whole of God's People (Mic 4:10 and Is 66:7-9). Her labour pains are of such dimensions that they can be likened to the suffering of a whole nation in need of God's deliverance (Is 7:16-18 and Jer 4:31). Yet she must be protected and hidden away by Yahweh while the great dragon that threatens her is vanquished (Is 27:1). In all of this, the Woman in her pregnancy and delivery stands as a God-given sign – higher than heaven and deeper than the underworld – that God's promises to David are sure and true (Is 7:14).

New facets of the Seer's awareness of Church are brought to the fore through this vision of the Woman. John has already shown us in his opening visions that the Church has both human and spiritual dimensions, but now he leads us one step further. By the Woman's apparition as a heavenly sign, John tells us that while, at one level, the Church is formed and acts in history, the Church just as truly belongs to eternal and celestial realms. In other words, the Church constitutes a mystical reality that is something more than the totality of its human members.[4] The great sign indicates a Church that embraces all of God's Chosen People, not just that phase of the People's history that begins with the coming of Jesus. The great ancestors, prophets, leaders and pious people of ancient Israel as well as the apostles, martyrs and faithful disciples of Christ in John's day can all identify themselves with this sun-bedecked figure and with the glory, tenderness and protection God bestows upon her. Any division between 'Israel' and 'Church' would be artificial and misleading for the Seer. There is but one Chosen People and John sees its reality in his vision of Daughter Zion.

---

4. The same sort of insight can be found expressed in different ways elsewhere in the New Testament, such as the image in Colossians and Ephesians of Christ as head of the Church. Paul's allegory in Galatians 4:22-31 speaks of the Church in a similar way to Revelation, as a heavenly reality that is not simply the composite of its members, and also uses the image of mother to do so.

The first lines of the Woman's story bring together contrasting aspects of her mystery. She is awe-inspiring, powerful, belonging to the eternal realms of heaven; but also endangered, suffering and in need of protection from a being that is – at least in some sense – lesser than herself. She is mother of the child destined to be ruler of the nations, yet she must live in the desert for her safety. While her son of destiny is brought to the throne of God, the Woman must continue to be threatened and to be victimised through her enemy's hostility against the rest of her children. The Woman inherits the ancient conflict between the serpent and the children of Eve that began soon after the world's creation. Like Eve's encounter with the serpent of Eden, the Woman's time of trial has cosmic consequences; but this time the Woman and her seed will have the final triumph.[5] For all of the contrasts, John gives us clear indications that a unified picture will emerge: the Woman and her children will be vindicated and victorious, even though they must endure much for three and a half years.

The Ancient Serpent

The Seer quickly introduces 'another sign', although he does not dignify this one by calling it 'great'. Mind you, it is striking enough for most of us and John does admit that – as dragons go – it can be called great. The Woman, however, remains the centre of attention for this chapter and the sign set most firmly before our eyes.

The dimensions and details of the Dragon's description are difficult to fathom; no artist's brush could adequately capture the fearsomeness that the Seer achieves with his few phrases. More striking still are the dimensions of the Dragon's malice and determination for evil. Rarely in our religious thinking do we even begin to think of Satan in these terms of might or sheer horror.

When John uses the dragon/serpent image, he delves deeply into the human psyche. Dragons and serpents play such important roles in the mythologies of the ancient cultures of different continents

---

5. The Seer designates the other children of the Woman as 'the rest of [the Woman's] seed' in 12:17 to link this passage to Genesis 3:15. In Genesis, of course, Eve's descendants are all of humanity, but this is not the case in Revelation. The children of the Woman of Revelation 12 are clearly identified in 12:17 as those who keep the commandments and bear testimony to Jesus. Daughter Zion represents a new beginning for humanity, a new ending for an ancient cosmic struggle.

The Great Sign (Rev 11:19–12:18)

that it is hard to avoid talking of a symbol that is archetypal, that seems to cross cultural barriers with amazing ease. Israel used this symbol too, and in doing so often spoke in mythological terms that would have been easily understood by neighbouring peoples. In some of the cultures to which Israel was heir, the dragon was a striking symbol for the forces of chaos. It lived in the sea (and at times was identified with the sea), constantly threatening the land and the human world that occupied it. The dragon sometimes stood for the dark primordial force that the creating god had to conquer in order to form the world. Although the dragon is not exactly a central figure in Israel's Scriptures, it has entered the biblical texts (and Jewish religious texts outside of the Bible), especially as Leviathan. Biblical references can be found in Job 41 or Isaiah 27:1 to Leviathan's unsurpassable might that only Yahweh can conquer.

Although John is undoubtedly using the biblical and mythical figure of Leviathan, he calls his Dragon by a different name: the Devil or Satan. We may not notice it, but in these titles the Seer points to the malice that drives the Dragon's actions. In the Greek in which John was writing, 'devil' means slanderer; similarly, 'Satan' in Hebrew means accuser. Like many biblical concepts, the idea of Satan had a long development over time. In parts of the Hebrew Bible, 'satan' seems to denote a function in the heavenly court – the one who brings charges and substantiates them, much like a Director of Public Prosecutions or a District Attorney does today. As time went on, this somewhat neutral picture faded and was replaced by a concept of vicious supernatural powers at enmity with God and humanity. The picture of Satan as personified supernatural evil is a familiar one to any reader of the New Testament, although we rarely see it portrayed with the unbridled force that John uses in Revelation 12.

John's Dragon is very much the Accuser. Its spite and venom are directed at the Woman and her children in the same way that its malice revolts against God. Yet the Dragon's role in Revelation cannot be reduced to a single function. The Dragon is the great leader of all supernatural evil, at the head of a whole band of warring angels. The Dragon still represents the chaos that wants to overthrow the divine rule and plan. The Dragon is behind all the forces with which the churches must contend – calling them up, orchestrating their actions, hoping to be the beneficiary of any success they may enjoy. Slander and accusation are still his weapons. Having failed with them in the celestial realms, the Dragon still attempts to destroy the Woman with the evil stream that pours from its mouth.

However powerful the Dragon appears, the Seer assures us that it is already defeated and cast down to the earth until its final destruction. The force and determination with which the Dragon attempts to devour and destroy are themselves but the violent thrashings of its death throes. Rejoicing over this victory can truly begin in heaven, but the day for pure rejoicing has not yet arrived for people on the earth. John warns his audience that the Dragon will try to make the most of the three and a half years remaining to it. And, as Revelation 12 shows, the Dragon's energy during its earthly exile will be aimed most directly at the Woman and her children.

Mother Zion

In the face of the drama that the Seer narrates, it would be easy to think that persecution and divine protection are the chief concerns the Seer wants to present to us in this chapter's treatment of Church. They are important parts of the picture, but John has shown them to us before. True, when the Seer situates the Church's trials in the cosmic struggle between Satan and God, he lifts another fold of the veil that fuzzes our normal perception of things. But as he shows us another aspect of what the Church must endure, the Seer also wants to tell us more about what the Church *is*. In order to delve more deeply into the reality of Church, John uses the well-established biblical image of Daughter Zion.

To learn that John shows us a vision of Daughter Zion in the Woman will not exactly excite most modern readers of the Apocalypse. The very phrase 'Daughter Zion' seems remote and antiseptic, a technical term that belongs in the mouths of biblical specialists. Those who previously associated the Woman of Revelation 12 with Mary might even feel somewhat aggrieved. Instead of a real human person with whom we can associate, with whom many Christians have a spiritual relationship, scholarship seems to be offering us an unfamiliar abstraction.

The Great Sign (Rev 11:19–12:18)

The first readers of the Apocalypse would have reacted quite differently. To them, Daughter Zion was a warm and meaningful symbol that captured much of the tenderness and warmth of Yahweh's relationship with Israel. Unlike the Jewish members of John's communities, we are not really used to thinking of sacred places as embodying a whole loving relationship between ourselves and the divine, nor are we at home with personifying a city (or nation or people) in anything other than fleeting superficial ways. Difficult as it is to enter someone else's way of thinking, it is even harder to appreciate the emotive associations that may be the central part of that thinking. But we need to try if we are to gain anything from the image of Daughter Zion in Revelation 12.

John's churches were part of the Greek-speaking world and they would have used the Scriptures in the Greek translation rather than in the Hebrew and Aramaic originals.[6] Sometimes that is significant, for the Greek translation of a passage can differ somewhat from the translations from the Hebrew that we are used to reading in our Bibles. If we want to discover some of the emotions that John and his people would have associated with the image of Daughter Zion, looking at the image in the psalms – prayers at the heart of the spiritual life of the ancient churches – can act as a first step. Psalm 87, for example, focuses on Daughter Zion; it is but one of many that celebrate the importance of Zion. The Greek version of it can be translated in this way:

> God's foundations are in place on the holy mountains.
> The Lord loves the gates of Zion
> more than all the tents of Jacob.
> Words filled with glory are spoken of you, City of God!
>
> I will call Rahab and Babylon to the minds of those that know me,
> even foreigners and Tyre and the people of Ethiopia –
> these were born there.
>
> 'Mother Zion!' each one will say,
> and each one was born in her.

---

6. While John uses the Greek translation (or Septuagint) in his work, there is strong evidence that he personally was familiar with the Hebrew and Aramaic as well.

> The Most High himself has built her foundation.
> The Lord shall record it in writing of the peoples.
>
> 'She is the home of these princes born in her' –
> Just so, the home of all those who rejoice is in you.

What this psalm celebrates is what John sees happening all around him. Peoples from foreign nations are being gathered into Israel, the Chosen People, through the mission of the Church. Even the nations that were formerly Israel's bitterest and most devastating enemies swell the influx. A sense of homecoming, welcome and celebration fills this psalm. Daughter Zion's embrace of her children passes on to them something of the tender love that she herself has received from God since the beginning.

The Greek version of Psalm 87 contains a phrase, 'Mother Zion', that is not to be found in the Hebrew text as it has come down to us. The phrase may be missing, but the idea is certainly there – as it is in other passages from the Hebrew Bible – and the idea of Zion's motherhood is a central part of the portrait of Daughter Zion that the author has painted in Revelation 12.

John is first shown Daughter Zion as she is about to give birth, a birth that takes place amidst her anguish and pain. Her labour occasions the appearance of the Dragon who is determined to destroy her child. Daughter Zion brings forth the Messiah, who is taken to heaven while she herself must remain on the earth as the target of the Dragon's ire. Once the divine protection has placed Daughter Zion safely in the desert, the Dragon's violent plans focus on her other children. Daughter Zion enters the narrative in the last pains of pregnancy, is depicted as mother of the Messiah, is hated by the Dragon for her motherhood, and the narrative leaves her (for the moment) by identifying her as the mother of all who keep the commandments and witness to Jesus. The new image that John wants us to keep in mind as we enter the second half of his work is not only Daughter Zion; she is Mother Zion.

If John's image of Daughter Zion as mother is to help us in our spiritual adventure, we need to work at comprehending and appreciating it. When we read any literary work from another time or culture, translating images can give us more headaches than translating words. We force our own cultural associations onto

The Great Sign (Rev 11:19–12:18)

texts and often end up hearing something that the original author never had in mind. We can be like the child whose favourite hymn was in honour of the church mascot, 'Gladly, the Cross-Eyed Bear' (a mishearing of 'Gladly the Cross I'd Bear'). Subconsciously we can substitute what is familiar for something that isn't really understood. What the author intended can never enter our heads, for its way is blocked by our false confidence that we have made perfect sense of what is before us.

The existence of learned volumes on the biblical books and long footnotes in study-Bibles is some indication of the problems biblical images like that of Daughter Zion pose. The Scriptures emerged in a variety of languages from an even broader spectrum of different times and cultures, every one of them as unfamiliar to us as the next. We can gain some insight into biblical images drawn from the natural world by visiting biblical lands (or even the local zoo). I can't stay in Ireland and get a real feeling for the desert, but that image was familiar and real for the biblical authors and their audiences. Lions appear in many of Israel's historical and prophetic books but never, thanks be to God, in my back garden. When biblical authors looked to nature as a mining place for images, they often dug in territory that is very unfamiliar to me. But at least I realise that it is unfamiliar.

If natural images pose problems, images drawn from the human world compound the problem – especially if I mistakenly assume that the image meant the same to the original author and audience as it does to me. For instance, to many people in Britain and Ireland, a Samaritan is a skilled volunteer who is at the other end of a telephone when someone needs a confidential conversation. The notion that many in Jesus' audiences would have bristled with bigotry against Samaritans is now a piece of specialised knowledge; the image has lost its punch. The word 'publican' that appeared often in older translations of the New Testament provides another example. As long as one remembered that it stood for 'tax collector', it didn't cause insurmountable difficulties. But that is not what the word means when we use it today. Now the word stands for one who runs a pub, and there isn't much overlap between the word's significance in contemporary speech and its significance in gospel translation. If a reader is not aware of the distinction, a strange misreading of the text is sure to follow.

These examples are relatively simple and their problems can be dispersed with a word or two of explanation. Two thousand years of social and cultural change produce much more complicated cases. Although we still have monarchs in some countries, the affirmation that 'Yahweh is king!' can never ring with the immediate overtones of glory and power with which it was once shouted in Israel's Temple. The kingship of Yahweh gives depth and momentum to so many texts in both testaments, including those concerned with the Kingdom of God, that any serious student of Scripture must make the effort to understand it with both head and heart. Images that are specifically male or female bring in concerns that are burning issues for both Church and society today. Consequently we can hear in them strong overtones that the original audiences would never have heard and that the authors never intended to make.

Some feel that the way out of this problem is to tone down the biblical images, even to make changes to the biblical text. It can be argued that there are circumstances which make this the best way forward, but it comes at a cost. Christians do not believe that the Scriptures are a collection of eternal divine truths loosely wrapped in human words that are secondary or incidental. The Word of God is expressed in the Scriptures in a type of incarnation, akin to the mysterious incarnation of Christ; driving a sharp wedge between Scripture's divine aspect and its human aspect ignores, perhaps even denies, the Spirit's action of speaking through the human authors. Radically modifying the imagery of the biblical text involves changing its human aspect, and thereby affecting the process of communicating the divine truth. One would have grounds to suspect that such modification is a sign that Scripture is no longer being respected as the Word of God.

Unfortunately, the very way in which images have been used over the years can so load an image with overtones that it becomes very difficult to rediscover its original focus. Sometimes this happens as a result of a transformation that occurs through social change, at other times through an unbalanced use of the image in the life of the Church. The image of judgment, for instance, can strike fear into the hearts of Christians; yet the image is often used in the Scriptures to inspire confidence and hope in the hearers. Centuries of badly placed emphasis – not only by preachers but also by poets and artists – have transformed this image into something that is nearly totally negative.

When we look at John's portrait of the Chosen People as Daughter Zion, these problems become very relevant. Some modern readers are immediately uncomfortable with any feminine image that was forged in a highly male-dominated society. Others will be tempted to transpose the more familiar image of Mother Church onto John's image of Daughter Zion. But the image of Mother Church invokes for some people a particular authoritarian model of motherhood that the Seer certainly didn't intend. The image of Mother Church has been damaged through misuse and can actually be a hindrance to anyone who wants to appreciate the image John has chosen.

Our reaction to John's image of Daughter Zion will be coloured by such things as our appreciation of Israel's Daughter Zion tradition, our own picture of motherhood or our personal experience of Church. Because of the cultural and historical gaps, the image does not immediately reverberate for us with the associations John would have liked it to have. Despite the problems, we need to recover John's image as one that will help us to fill out our own perception of Church. We can begin by identifying a few aspects of John's picture that reveal what the image meant to him.

First, Daughter Zion appears with celestial dignity from heaven, the home of God. The Seer graphically lifts the Church from the theatre of its earthly existence to show that the Church has an eternal and mystical relationship with God. We see here the truth that is expressed in many different ways throughout the Scriptures: God *loves* the Church. Sun, moon and stars serve as mere baubles in God's action of bestowing tokens of love upon beloved Daughter Zion.

Second, Daughter Zion brings forth the promised ruler. All the promises made to Israel belong to her and she carries them in her own person wherever she goes. She herself is the great sign of their reliability and she proves them true in the act of giving the Messiah to the world.

Third, Daughter Zion suffers. She suffers because of the nearly transcendent power of evil that directs all its might against her, but she also suffers as mother in order that the Messiah might be brought forth. Her very suffering, therefore, is fruitful and productive and a necessary part of her motherhood.

Fourth, Daughter Zion enjoys the solicitous, caring love of God. The divine love provides her with a place of safety and bears her there on eagle's wings. Even the forces of God's creation, recognising Daughter Zion as belonging to God as creation itself does, help her by protecting her from the Dragon's attempt to sweep her away. Daughter Zion's circumstances may not strike us as ideal, but they still provide Daughter Zion with a haven for the three and a half years.

Fifth, Daughter Zion must be in the desert. Israel's Scriptures recognise that the desert is harsh and trying, but some passages speak of the desert as a place where people can be in the intimate presence of God. Daughter Zion may have left her splendid home in the heavens, but she is still very much with God. She waits there, nourished and protected, knowing that she will eventually be called from this desert – just as Israel was brought from the Sinai desert to enter the home promised them by God.

Finally, Daughter Zion is the mother of all God's faithful people. Her mothering has brought them to life and trained them with love. Her children share her suffering and are drawn into the cosmic struggle that she must endure. But they do not suffer as bystanders caught up in a battle that is not theirs. Because they belong to Daughter Zion as her children, they cannot disassociate themselves from what she endures. Their love for Daughter Zion and her love for them necessarily involves them in her tribulation.

The Seer's vision of Daughter Zion calls us to see the Church as something noble and dignified. The Woman's celestial garb makes her shine with a divine light – not a light that springs from some divinity of her own person, but the light of God's love that surrounds and embraces her. As Church, we are not only called by God to share in the divine plan; we are the centre of God's plan, the chosen object of divine love, the splendid focus of God's desire. God delights in the Church and works mightily to enrich and beautify us.

The Church is destined to bring the world its Messiah. Through the promises entrusted to the Church in the days of ancient Israel, God gave humanity a beacon of hope and guidance. Daughter Zion's faithfulness to God and God's faithfulness to Daughter Zion result in nothing less than the coming of the Messiah. We are reminded that the Church is still the bearer of these promises and hopes for the world. The Church appears and acts in the world of humanity, still pregnant with its Saviour.

Through her suffering and tribulation, Daughter Zion fulfils her role in the divine plan, and suffering continues to form a part of the Church's destiny. The part suffering plays in John's description of Daughter Zion can help us to see that the Church's suffering is productive, even necessary. Yet the suffering can only be viewed in light of the caring love of God that accompanies it. The temptations always to fight back, to reject the pain that belonging to God involves, to think of times of trial as outside the blueprint God has for the Church must be resisted. Instead of resistance and rejection, the Church's proper response to tribulation is John's great virtue of endurance, based in the trust that what can appear meaningless and unnecessary can, in fact, be pushing the divine plan along. In our desert, we do encounter trial. But we also find the place where we can encounter God and experience the depths of the divine love for us.

John's use of the Daughter Zion image calls the Church to rediscover in its life and mission all the joys of motherhood. Through the image itself and the biblical passages in which it is rooted, the Church can see its vocation to be life-bearing and nurturing, welcoming and embracing, providing a true home for all peoples, tenderly loving each member of the family as truly as any other, privileged to share with God a parental relationship with each disciple. This image should help anyone involved in the leadership of the Church to critique those aspects of Church life that project a different image, that distort Daughter Zion into a parody of motherhood. Unfortunately, human parents can be demanding and overbearing, cold and stern – and the image of Mother Church can recall the image of parents who do not want their children to mature. The biblical image of Daughter Zion challenges Church leaders in particular to make Daughter Zion's children feel cherished as members of God's family, to have the security of finding a true home and a loving family. In many of the texts from the Hebrew Bible associated with this image, we get a sense of Daughter Zion's delight in her children (and of their delight in her). If church leaders have been given a special share in the demanding task of nourishing and guiding Daughter Zion's children, they are also blessed with a call to share in her delight and joy. If this sense of motherly delight is missing, it might be an indication that wrong approaches have been taken to the task of nourishing and guiding as well.

As John moves on with his vision, he leaves the Woman in the desert. Some readers of the Apocalypse get the feeling that the Woman is no longer of interest to the Seer, but they are wrong. We will see Daughter Zion again, even though we may not recognise her at first sight. But, for the moment, she has played her part in the story. She has given us a further understanding of what being Church entails: the overpowering dignity that God has bestowed upon us, our part in the cosmic warfare, the tender love of God for us, and the fruitful motherhood that brings the hopes of Israel to their fulfilment.

John has tilted the mirror that he holds up in front of us to give us a slightly different perspective; by letting us see ourselves as Daughter Zion, he has told us a bit more about who and what we are. And, lest we be daunted by the awesomeness of what we are about to see, John has strengthened us with the reminder of our own awesomeness contained in the great sign of Daughter Zion. Now John is about to lift another bit of the veil and show us the spiritual adventure in which we are already involved, whether we realised it or not. Daughter Zion's story is not finished yet.

Questions for Reflection and Prayer

1. The Seer does not invite us as individuals into his spiritual adventure; his spirituality is Church-centred. Can you identify some implications for the churches today which arise from this fact?

2. The Woman Clothed with the Sun is presented by the Seer as a great sign, and in terms that would have been easy for first-century Christians to recognise as a symbol of the Church, the

The Great Sign (Rev 11:19–12:18)

People of God. What are the chief clues to her identity that John gives in Revelation 12?

3. The Daughter Zion image has deep roots in the consciousness of Ancient Israel. Which aspects of this image were particularly significant for John the Seer? Which aspects do you find encouraging?

4. John's use of the Daughter Zion image calls the Church to rediscover in its life and mission all the joys of motherhood. How do you think this is possible in today's world? Identify some ways in which you can personally participate in realising the Church's vocation to be life-bearing and nurturing, welcoming and embracing?

7

Unmasking the Pretenders

Revelation 13:1-17:18

When opinion pollsters get religious, they ask questions like 'Do you believe in God?' 'Do you believe in an afterlife?' 'Do you believe in the devil?' You can hardly expect pollsters to be good theologians, but I still feel a bit bemused by the last question. I know what it is to believe in God. It involves love, trust, obedience and surrender. Given this understanding, I don't think that I want to meet the person who 'believes in' the devil.

There is a second objection that one can make to the pollsters' question: Why 'the devil'? Why not 'devils'? Although we talk about 'the devil' (often with a capital 'D'), Jews and Christians traditionally think of a number of these spirits, not just one. Any good cartoon of hell will bear me out.

I admit that this second objection is somewhat frivolous, and I doubt if it will result in a revised list of religious questions in the next opinion poll, but it does touch on the narrative of the Apocalypse. The Seer has described Satan for us with unsurpassable force. So much evil and hatred is gathered up into this figure that we might be surprised that there is any evil and hatred left to make a second figure. Yet, as the Dragon stands by the sea, a second evil being rises with as many heads and horns and even more crowns. Not too far behind comes a third evil being, and we could well feel that we are beginning to lose count. The Dragon and the Beasts of Revelation do not fit in quickly with the images of the chief devil and his less powerful minions that we find in art and folklore. We immediately recognise that these Beasts are forces to be reckoned with, just as the Dragon itself is.

Evaluating Roman Rule

We noted in the last chapter how the Seer used the biblical figure of Leviathan to portray the Dragon. In describing the Beast from the Sea, John has once again turned to the Hebrew Bible to provide himself with language suitable to the task. The seventh chapter of Daniel – a passage that John has already referred to in his opening vision of the Son of Man – describes four beasts rising from the sea, each one different from the others and each one a destroyer. Between them, Daniel's beasts had attributes of lions, bears, eagles and leopards; the fourth beast even had ten horns like Revelation's Beast from the Sea. The Book of Daniel used these beasts as symbols of the four empires that had conquered and oppressed Judah[1] and whose seemingly mighty rule was destined to pass and give way to God's Kingdom. Anyone in the Seer's audience familiar with the Book of Daniel would have an immediate sense of what John is getting at: here is a force as powerful and as destructive as the four evil empires of Israel's past rolled into one. When John tells of the Beast from the Sea, his audience knows that he has had a vision of the Roman Empire, even though no name appears in the text.[2]

We stand at some distance in time from the days when Rome dominated world affairs and impinged on many matters of everyday life. All the same, educated people today often know enough about Rome to form personal opinions about the Romans, perhaps even about their Empire. We are certainly more likely to have personal opinions about the Roman people than we are to have about the Babylonians, Medes or Persians – and perhaps not all that surprisingly. After all, the whole Western world is the cultural descendant of ancient Rome. We might think of the Romans as refined because of their art and literature, or we might think them as barbaric because of their militarism and gruesome entertainments; but we tend to have some feeling about them, even if an ambivalent one.

Since Rome and its rule enters the New Testament in different ways, its pages sometimes give us an opportunity to glance at the great political entity of the empire through contemporary, non-Roman eyes. If we think of the different reactions in first century

1. The attributes of the beasts in Daniel are drawn from traditional symbols for the Babylonians, the Medes, the Persians and the Greeks. They are meant to form a crescendo in Daniel's visions to highlight the pinnacle of oppression that the Jews had to endure under their Hellenistic overlords, especially in the days of Antiochus IV when these visions were written.

2. The Beast (Behemoth) in Job 40:15-24 is linked with Leviathan, not only in that book but also in Jewish tradition and folklore. The Seer shows that he is aware of this connection by linking the Dragon and the Beast(s) in his narrative vision, but the beasts of Daniel 7 are far more influential upon his symbolism than is the Beast of Job 40.

Palestine alone, we can see the variety of ways of viewing the Roman Empire. Rome made its presence felt in a province through its resident authority (such as proconsul or governor), its tax collectors and its occupation troops. On the whole, the Jewish people did not exactly welcome their Roman overlords. For their part, the Romans knew that trouble could break out at any time; there were enough skirmishes and rebellions to remind any Roman of that possibility.

Then there was the religious question. The Romans found Judaism baffling; they couldn't really comprehend that their very presence was an affront to many religious Jews. Images of emperors with reference to their divine dignity and the eagle on the Roman military standards were condemned by the Jews as idolatry. Even to have someone other than an Israelite exercising power over the nation of Israel was seen by some Jews as an infringement of God's sole right to sovereignty over the Chosen People. Against all that, there were people that the Romans would have found more reasonable. Herod, his family, the chief priests and the Sadducees all seemed willing to accept the situation as it was and to form realistic working relationships to everyone's advantage. But, all in all, Judea was a powder keg which would explode in the first century and beyond.

If our main view of the Roman Empire is formed from the standpoint of a first century Palestinian Jew, then we could well have a picture of a number of oppressed and occupied nations groaning under the Roman yoke. In fact, even though Roman rule undoubtedly caused resentment in many quarters, there were places in which it was positively welcomed. In many regions Roman rule had brought peace where local rivalries had caused decades of struggle and war. Rome had brought economic advantage to its provinces in times of tranquillity and humanitarian relief in times of disaster. Rome showed respect for its provinces, their leading families and their traditions, insofar as these did not detract from a province's integration into Rome's Empire.

The evidence shows that Asia Minor and its cities held a very favourable view of being part of the Empire. Roman rule was seen by these cities as benevolent, and membership of the empire was something to be proud of. Few places were as enthusiastic about

Unmasking the Pretenders (Rev 13:1-17:18)

honouring Rome and its emperors with temples and sacrifices. Roman rule was received very differently in Ephesus than it was in Jerusalem. For a leading citizen of the province of Asia, loyalty to your city meant being proud of its close links with Rome. For many Jews, being proud of your nationality meant dreaming of the day when Roman rule would be broken.

Was there a specifically Christian view on Roman rule? We encounter a whole spectrum of views within the New Testament itself. Some texts seem to indicate a general suspicion of political power and its structures. Such an attitude is certainly there in the background of Luke 4:6 when Satan boasts that the kingdoms of the world belong to him and that he gives them to whomever he wishes; the reader of Luke cannot help but be reminded of the identification of Satan as 'the Prince of this world' in the Fourth Gospel. Yet the image of Satan as the one in political control contrasts with Paul's assertion (in Romans 13:1-7) that all earthly authority comes from God and that disciples must respect and obey it as part of discipleship. A theme that runs through Acts of the Apostles is that the empire has nothing to fear from Christians and that the empire and its authorities have actually been helpful to the Church in its task of spreading Christ's Good News. Honour and obedience to the emperor are explicity demanded of disciples in 1 Peter 2:13-17. If there would have been a debate in the first century Church on the topic 'Roman Empire: Force for Good or Evil?', it looks like there wouldn't have been a problem in finding prominent figures to fill either team.

The Seer disclosed his own reaction to the empire when he used the beasts of Daniel 7 to portray it. He acknowledged that his opinion is far from the popular one; most people are happy to follow the Beast and worship it. John was not surprised by the world's regard for the Beast from the Sea, but he cannot share it now that he has been shown the Beast for what it really is. The Empire Beast is certainly mighty, but its might stems from the power of the Dragon. Its crowns and horns indicate its success and its true authority over nations and peoples, but the Beast has overstepped its boundaries by demanding nothing less than human worship. The Beast utters blasphemies in its claims to divine power and it declares war on God's People (again, with some success as

13:7 notes). John, unlike many of his contemporaries, has seen the Beast in its true colours.

Rome the Maker of Martyrs?

From our viewpoint, we might be surprised that John's reaction wasn't the universal judgment of Christians on Rome. After all, weren't the Roman soldiers of this time engaged in hunting down disciples and making martyrs of them? Hadn't the Empire made it a capital offence to believe in Jesus? The real situation in the first century was more complex than that. There were certainly persecutions and martyrs in the Church's early days. Peter and Paul were among the great number who died in a persecution in Rome under Nero, but simple belief in Christ did not provide the grounds for their death sentences. The martyrs of Nero's persecution were executed on a trumped-up charge that Christians had started the fire in which a great part of the city of Rome was destroyed. Since suspicion had turned on Nero himself, he badly needed a scapegoat and he found one in the local Christians. In a sense, the death sentences passed on these first Roman martyrs belonged to the field of local news for the city of Rome; these executions were not part of some Empire-wide attempt to eradicate a new religion.

Nero's action may also have given us the wrong impression that persecution in New Testament times was always the action of the Roman emperors and Roman law. This simply was not the case. Acts of the Apostles, for instance, relates stories of martyrdom and of attempted martyrdom – but nowhere was Roman law to blame for these hostile actions. Instead, the hostility sprang from local groups and local interests. Roman law certainly made martyrs, especially in the second and third centuries, but most of the martyrs of New Testament times received their crowns in other ways.

Historians also point out that the age of the martyrs was not one long period of constant and universal persecution. The martyrs' graves in the catacombs (which themselves are later than the New Testament period) were carefully marked and greatly venerated, but they form a very small minority of burials. Even when being a Christian in itself constituted a civil offence, church leaders and other disciples were usually left alone except when local circumstances made it expedient to take action against them. Generally speaking, the persecutions that made martyrs tended to happen locally and sporadically, even if the laws were there in the background to enable an interested party to bring charges when it suited, either against an individual Christian or the whole local church. Most disciples of the first three centuries went about their daily business and formed part of normal society, even if they practised a religion that was not considered respectable. Contrary to the popular picture, the early Christians did not spend their days and nights huddled together in the catacombs nervously listening for the sound of soldiers on the hunt.

That doesn't mean that disciples didn't have to take care. The danger of arrest, imprisonment, banishment and even death was never all that far away, and Christians devised their systems of discretion and secrecy for their own self-preservation. It could make a difference who was emperor at a given time. The reigns of some emperors (such as the second century rulers Antonius Pius, Marcus Aurelius and Commodus) were known to be times of persecution. On the other hand, Trajan and Hadrian – also emperors during the second century – held back some of their local governors from going overboard on arresting and punishing disciples, and some third century emperors could even be described as friendly towards the Church.

For many years people took it for granted that the Seer wrote in a time of great persecution under the emperor Domitian. Domitian's name had been joined in tradition to those of Nero, Decius, Valerian and Diocletian as emperors who masterminded onslaughts against the Christian faith. Yet the historical evidence just doesn't bear this out. There were certainly martyrs made during Domitian's reign, but they seem to have been relatively few when compared to other times. There isn't much evidence to show that Domitian had personally tried to turn the might of the Empire against the Christians. When the evidence is weighed up, it seems that the tradition that portrays Domitian as a great persecutor is based on very little. It could actually have sprung from the tradition that locates the writing of the Apocalypse in his reign. The Seer's picture of the glorious band of martyrs was interpreted as a reflection of unusually horrendous persecution in progress at the time of writing, and Domitian (who certainly had his faults as emperor) received the reputation of being an insatiable enemy of the Church.

Something interesting happens to our reading of Revelation when we take the historians seriously. All of a sudden, the Seer's portrayal of the empire as a force at war with the Church is no longer one that all of his readers would immediately recognise. John could have been trying to paint a picture that would open their eyes to something they had never seen before. As residents in the cities of Asia Minor, many in John's churches could well have agreed whole-heartedly with their compatriots that Rome was a benevolent power that brought peace and prosperity to the region. They might well have argued that belonging to the empire was a good thing. Certainly it is likely that many of them would personally have benefited from their city's links with Rome. John's vision of the empire as a beast would not have rested easily with them. The force with which the Seer attempts to show them this side of the empire could itself indicate John's awareness that many in his audience held a view very different from his own.

Of course, we can't be sure where the first readers of Revelation stood on this whole question of the empire. Our very uncertainty actually helps us in taking John's vision seriously: we cannot simply pigeonhole John's viewpoint on political realities as something that only applies to an ancient force that was violently and determinedly set on the destruction of the Church. John could also have been speaking about an empire that would have struck many Christians as benevolent and beneficial. When he speaks of the Beast from the Sea, John intends to speak specifically of the Roman Empire, but he knows that there is something about this beast that can be applied to other situations and other empires.[3] Any political structure, any political power must be examined to ensure that it doesn't match the portrait John has painted.

---

3. By using the imagery of Daniel, the Seer is locating the evil of the Roman Empire in a whole line of evil that also involves the Babylonians, Medes, Persians and Seleucid Empires. John is not rejecting that chain of oppression but extending it. By his portrayal of the Empire, he shows the latest and most horrible link in the chain. In this context it is interesting to note that the Greek of 13:1 could also be translated 'I saw a beast that *keeps rising* from the sea.' John might have been using this slight nuance to indicate that he knows that the political manifestation of evil doesn't begin or end with the rise and fall of Rome.

The Beast from the Earth

Ancient lore often connected the forces of chaos with the sea, and John echoes these traditions in showing us the Empire Beast rising from the sea. That there is another beast that arises 'from the earth'[4] might have a different significance. The Empire Beast arrives from abroad; this Second Beast finds its origins closer to home.[5]

The Second Beast has close connections to the first one and could even be seen as being at its service. The language John uses of the Second Beast shows that it performs the role of false prophet, working wonders and leading people astray; he even refers to this beast as the false prophet (19:20). Although the letters to the seven churches indicate that false prophets were at work within the communities, the Second Beast is obviously something more than just a collective symbol for such people. The Second Beast is something far greater; it controls everyday affairs and has the universal worship of the Empire Beast as its objective. The Second Beast represents, at least in part, the imperial cult that was very popular in John's neck of the Empire.

With our mental division between religion and politics, the whole notion of an imperial cult doesn't make a lot of sense. For much of antiquity, however, there were strong links between religion and the state. Gods were national gods and religions didn't cross national boundaries easily. In the ancient world, individual salvation was not the motivation behind religious practice. Instead sacrifices were carried out more in the national interest. Good rule, national prosperity and military success were the fruits that state religions hoped to harvest. On the other hand, individual concerns were far from irrelevant to ancient religious practices. Men and women hoped for great blessings from their gods and sometimes ancient pagan prayers demonstrate what we might call a personal, even mystical spirituality; however the main concerns of public religion always centred on the nation and its well-being. When we understand this mentality, the imperial cult begins to become a bit

---

4. The phrase could also be translated 'from the land'. The Greek word used here for 'earth' also means land and is often used for a national territory, whereas the English word 'earth' usually has more global connotations.

5. Perhaps John is referring to the part the people of Asia Minor had in the imperial cult's origins. The Second Beast is no foreign invader but something native to the cities to which the Seer was writing.

more reasonable. Add to all that the tradition to be found in Asia Minor, as in other parts of the East, that the king's unique relationship to the gods bestowed a divine aura upon his own person, and emperor worship becomes easier to understand.

The imperial cult could be called the worship of power. Since we have some feeling for people worshipping the sun and other powers of nature, we shouldn't find it all that strange that people have also felt moved to worship political power as well. When people in the provinces of the Roman Empire worshipped the goddess Roma, they intended to worship the supernatural power that had made itself manifest in the benevolent strength of Roman rule.[6] Leading citizens from the cities of Rome's provinces were the ones who, in the first place, had come up with the idea of worshipping the emperor as a god. When their desire was put before him, Augustus refused the request and only permitted the worship of his 'genius' – the guardian spirit that supernaturally guided him in his function as emperor – and that was only allowed if it went hand in hand with the worship of Roma. Since dead emperors were often declared by the Roman Senate to have become gods, and since some living emperors (like Caligula and Domitian) liked the idea that they were divine even before their deaths, things did not develop quite as neatly as Augustus might have intended. To some people, including a few emperors, the living emperor was simply a living god.

The imperial cult did remain true to the prescription of Augustus in at least one respect: its honouring of the emperor continued to be linked to the worship of the goddess Roma. The cult was truly a religion; it had its priesthood, its temples, its prescribed rituals and its public ceremonies. Prominent citizens strove to be listed among the cult's priests, and cities competed for the honour of having the cult's leading priesthood and temple of the region. Being involved in the imperial cult could be beneficial, if not vital, to one's financial health. The cult formed a real part of the public structures, buildings and life of the cities in Asia Minor. The festivals and public liturgies of the imperial cult would have impinged on the lives of Jews or Christians living in first century Pergamum or Ephesus even more than Christmas affects non-Christians living in

6. The goddess Roma seems to have been created for the benefit of the provincials. Her temples already appear in the provinces during the days of the Republic, but there is no evidence for worship of her in Rome itself until later.

the West today. The imperial cult's links to the affairs of government didn't mean that it was a drab, civil service type of operation; at least in some times and places the imperial cult was celebrated with splendour and real religious fervour. And it attracted its share of religious fraud too. Bogus miracles and machinery to make statues move and talk were not unknown in Rome's imperial cult.

We can call the Second Beast 'the Cult Beast'. For John, the Cult Beast embodies the whole religious system of the imperial cult as well as the individuals (including emperors) behind it – just as the Empire Beast embodies the Roman Empire. The relationship between these two Beasts and the Dragon has led some to talk of an 'Unholy Trinity'. That is not a bad way to think of these three forces, as long as we do not impose too much of our Christian theology about the Trinity onto John's picture. The Dragon flatters itself by trying to imitate God's powerful yet largely unseen presence in the human world, while the two Beasts are more directly experienced as the threesome work away to establish their dark dominion.

The characteristics of the Empire Beast and the Cult Beast show that both of these figures are a type of collage that includes individual actions and historical figures as well as systems. The link with the emperor Nero is particularly strong and deserves the attention of any reader of the Apocalypse. Popular lore had turned the historical Nero into a symbol for all the evil and danger that could threaten the quiet life or the civilised world. There were popular beliefs that his suicide attempt was really unsuccessful, or that he had come to life again, or that he was organising hostile forces to take over the world. Revelation reflects these rumours in the Empire Beast's head that had survived a mortal wound. Six hundred and sixty-six – the famous number of the Beast in 13:18 – is a type of code for 'Nero Caesar' derived from a system of adding up the numerical values assigned to the letters of a person's name.[7] The incorporation of Nero lore into the picture of these

---

7. John obviously intended this number to be pondered. One of the interesting aspects of it emerges when the significance of seven is taken into account. Since 7 is a number that represents completeness – and can have overtones of a divine perfection – and 3 also can represent the fullness of expression, three 6s have a sinister tinge. The number '666' connotes something just short of the full expression of divine perfection (which would be '777'), near enough to fool many people.

Beasts gives them an aura of supernatural horror. John seems to be saying to his audience that anything terrifying and threatening, all depravity and vileness, everything capable of inspiring fear and dread is there to be found in the empire and its cult.

Since the seven letters indicate that some in John's communities were not as committed about keeping their distance from pagan worship as John was, we might assume that there were some disciples who didn't see all that much harm in the imperial cult, just as today there are many sincere and committed Christians who see little harm in dabbling in astrology. In cases where rejection of the imperial cult infringed on one's involvement in society and commerce (as John implies in 13:16-17), the temptation must have been very strong indeed. If John's portrayal of the two Beasts hasn't convinced them, he has yet another vision to show them.

The Great Harlot and her Allurements

Even many who are unfamiliar with much of the Apocalypse have heard of the 'Whore of Babylon' (Rev 17). She does not appear in the Apocalypse as part of some campaign that the Seer is waging against selling sexual favours (although we may presume that John was hardly approving of such practices). The prostitution which is such a strong element in the description of the Great Harlot evokes an image of prostitution and adultery familiar to his audience from the writings of the prophets, an image that spoke forcefully of Israel's idolatry and unfaithfulness to Yahweh.

Prostitution was nearly the natural choice whenever an image for Israel's unfaithfulness was needed. In the days of the prophets, the Canaanite fertility cult and its worship of Baal had posed the main threat to Israel's worship of Yahweh as their only God. The rituals of Baal involved what scholars call cultic prostitution, the semi-magical practice of inducing the god to grant fertility to his land through sexual acts performed with men and women chosen for the purpose. In the days of the great prophets, prostitution was not only a figurative way of speaking for turning to false gods – it was also a literal description of what these unfaithful people were actually doing.

There was another side to the coin, however, and it was one that made the image useful even for idolatry that did not involve cultic prostitution. Just as a married person who resorts to prostitutes offends against the sacredness of the relationship of marriage, so those who engaged in idolatry insult and debase the unique relationship between Israel and Yahweh. The prophetic image of prostitution insists upon the worth of what idolatry rejects, the loving, exclusive and intimate relationship into which God's People have been brought. What people have chosen for themselves by turning to false gods is something filthy, tawdry and cheap. They have ceased to quest for God in their religion. Instead they use a religion based on their passions to try and gain benefits that are self-centred – success for themselves, vengeance on their enemies, good luck, and anything else that belongs only to this world.

Any mental image one might have of prostitutes as figures who are exploited by their clients and by those who control them does not apply to the Great Harlot of Revelation. *She* is the one in control, a person of great wealth living in tremendous luxury. Nor is the Great Harlot without her attractions; John admits his own initial fascination with her in 17:6. The Great Harlot is impressive, powerful and truly has much to offer those who approach her. The Great Harlot is Roma – city, empire and goddess enshrined in the temples of the imperial cult – and the vision shows her as holding all the riches of commerce and political control that have lured so many nations to yield themselves to her.[8]

Comparisons, they say, are odious – and that is exactly why John wants us to make them here. John has already shown us a very impressive woman in Revelation 12, and the Great Harlot is no match for her. The Great Harlot may be dressed in the luxuries that the world can offer, but what is that compared to the celestial splendour of Daughter Zion? Petty kings may flock to the Great Harlot, but Daughter Zion is the mother of One that will rule all the peoples of the world. Daughter Zion gives life to her children, while the Great Harlot takes life and makes herself drunk on the

---

8. Although we can make a distinction in English between Rome the city and Roma the goddess, Latin and Greek do not. The same name stood for both and John seems to be using the easy flow between the two ideas of Roma as city and Roma as worshipped in the imperial cult. Even though John calls the Great Harlot the 'Whore of Babylon', he shows that 'Babylon' really stands for Rome by decoding some of the symbolism in 17:9-10. Babylon was used as a symbolic name for Rome (see 1 Peter 5:13) and the word conjures up images of God's People living in exile under the domination of pagans.

blood of God's People. Daughter Zion belongs to God and appears from the realms of the divine dwelling. The Great Harlot is seated on the Empire Beast and dwells in the realms of the 'Unholy Trinity'. She represents their ridiculous attempt to fill the place that can only belong to the Woman Clothed with the Sun. Even though the Great Harlot enjoys her moment of glory, in the workings of the divine plan the Harlot must go; she must yield all things to Daughter Zion. When that moment comes, all her apparent success will be seen as the sham it really is. Even the allegiance of her clients will turn to hostility and violent rejection.

John reveals the Great Harlot to his audience in her true colours, and the picture is not pretty. Yet there is something about her that John knows is attractive to many in his churches. Given the sexual overtones of the image that the Seer has chosen, we might expect some symbolic reference to the Great Harlot's physical beauty. However, her attractions are described in terms of power and the wealth of commerce – the very aspects of Roman rule that most benefited wealthy provincial cities. The imperial cult provided an open door for individuals to share fully the benefits that Rome had brought to their municipalities, and 13:16-17 implies that those who kept away from the imperial cult did so to their personal loss. Yet the contrasts John makes between the Great Harlot and Daughter Zion highlight the black-and-white choice that is before his audience: they cannot belong to Daughter Zion and the Lamb and at the same time be clients of the Great Harlot.

There is another way in which the figures of Daughter Zion and Roma overlap: they are both strongly associated with worship. Given the Seer's obvious concern with that aspect of Christian life, we would be foolish to overlook it. Of course Daughter Zion herself was not worshipped, but as the chosen location for Yahweh's Temple the image of Daughter Zion evoked pictures of God's People gathered in the celebrations and festivals. It evoked echoes of hymns and musical instruments making joyful noises in praise of the Almighty, and memories of pilgrimages, processions, sacrifices and heart-felt pleas for divine help. Daughter Zion was where Israel's worship of God blossomed most abundantly and fragrantly. On the other hand, many in first century Asia Minor flocked to the worship of Roma and made pilgrimages to her temples. Roma was held up to them in the imperial cult as one worthy of their devotion and adoration. The Great Harlot's success or failure in her rivalry with Daughter Zion will be shown in the choice of worship that John's hearers make. They can either join in the choirs of Daughter Zion or sing in the temples of the imperial cult; but they can't do both. The times of choir practice definitely clash!

The Great Liberation of Israel

John insists on unmasking Rome and its empire despite the resistance that his message would receive from some of his hearers. He stubbornly maintains that the Empire is not benevolent and beneficial and that the imperial cult is not harmless. Empire and cult represent the darkest forces of Satan at work in the world. They are trying to usurp the very place of God with their pretensions to divinity. Even if some Christians don't see it, there is such a basic conflict between these forces and God that the Dragon and the Beasts will always be at war with those who belong to God.

We have spent so long considering the two Beasts that John's constant concern with God's People might have slipped a bit from sight. The Seer hasn't forgotten about it, we may be sure. In chapter fourteen John shows us the Lamb and his followers at home with Daughter Zion. The picture is unquestionably idealised and poetic. Since the picture depends on aspects of ritual purity, and since we tend to be unfamiliar with the very concept of ritual purity (as well as with the details of its demands), we lose the impact of John's description. The group surrounding the Lamb in Revelation 14 is described in terms like those used in Psalm 24 of a person ready to enter the Temple. John is telling us that the Lamb has prepared his companions and they are now ready for being brought into God's presence.

Yet God's People still have a distance to go before they finish their journey. They are in exile under the oppression of hostile powers that claim their own divinity and bring tribulation upon the Chosen People. The situation is much like that of the ancient Israelites in Egypt: a people in captivity, toiling under a pretender who is venerated as a god. The victory for Israel could only be won through a war between divinities. As God once conquered the false

Pharaoh-god, now the same battle must rage against the false deities of Dragon and Beasts if God's People are to be saved. The Egyptian exodus was a skirmish by comparison with the warfare that is now necessary; as we see in 16:13-14, this war not only involves Egypt but also all the nations of the earth that can be summoned by the Dragon and the Beasts.

The seven final plagues of chapters fifteen and sixteen echo the plagues that Yahweh brought upon Egypt in the exodus story, with overwhelming scenes appropriate to warfare raging between divine figures. As in the exodus story, there is no weapon fired back towards heaven except stubbornness. Yet these scenes are not simply part of the warfare for the Seer. He has brought us back to the workings of his heavenly liturgy. The Song of Moses[9] is sung as both a reminder and a celebration of God's past victories, but the song of the Lamb is added to it in 15:3-4 to celebrate the victory that is about to come. The plagues are carried in bowls by white-robed angels, just as white-robed priests carried sacred bowls containing blood and ashes when they ministered at the great sacrifices of the Jerusalem Temple. The victory in this war is the result of the Lamb's sacrifice, and the worship of God's People – both on earth and in the heavenly Sanctuary – accompanies the victory and participates in it. As the Seer indicates in 14:7-12, whether one has joined in the worship of God or been a participant in the worship of the Empire Beast determines whether this victory is good news or not. Once more the Seer reminds us that our worship makes history, unfolds its workings and ultimately shows whether the individual is on the victorious side or not.

Do Beasts Still Lurk?

In the introduction to this book, I referred to some people who have a certain fascination with the Apocalypse, especially to those who like to read it while holding a newspaper in the other hand. Not having tried it for myself, I can't say exactly how much fun there is in forcing the details of these bleaker visions of John's into identikit pictures of modern figures and events. But it does seem to give some people a high, and it can certainly become an obsession.

John did want his original audiences to make connections

---

9. See Exodus 15.

between parts of his images and their contemporary world, but sadly he made no provision for us to do the same. Yet the Seer is conscious that he is not just speaking about matters that are provincial and current. He is also talking about threats, battles, tribulations and allurements that are manifestations of something cosmic, something that will keep showing itself throughout that penultimate three and a half year period.

John undoubtedly intends us to follow his lead in interpreting the world around us so that our loyalty to God and the Lamb is not weakened by foolish loyalties given to lesser things. Yet we are rightly nervous about doing so since we no longer have the sure guidance or clear precision that the Seer could claim on the basis of his visionary experience. When we, as Church, apply what John is telling us about his world to our own, we can use only the broadest sweeps of John's pictures to guide us. Otherwise we will find ourselves constructing an outlandish fantasy in which modern events and figures prance about in fancy dress stolen from figures that are only to be found in John's late first century world.

All the same, John leaves us with quite a few points to ponder. His portrait of the Empire Beast should undermine any Christian's unreflective approval of powerful political structures as unalloyed forces for good. There is much about superpowers, for instance, that commends them to people of good will. In the days of the Cold War, it was easy to identify the forces of democracy with the side of the angels and to identify the forces of communism with the unleashed power of evil. The atheism central to Marxist philosophy served as enough indication to most Christians that communist governments were to be objects of suspicion. Many thought there was a flip-side to that particular coin; for them 'democracy' represented everything good and pleasing to God in world affairs. John's vision warns us against the dangers of such easy identification. The preservation of democracy was often used as the excuse for militarism and ignoring horrendous violations of human rights, including many different kinds of violation of the very right to life.

The ending of the Cold War has reduced the temptation to award such undiscerning loyalty to a political system, yet the need remains for Christians to critique those political realities to which they feel most attached and with which they can most easily identify. Perhaps John's vision of the Empire Beast gives us an even wider warning: if the Kingdom has not yet come in its fullness, if God's will is not fully at work in the world and its political workings, then the Christian must see that there is a limit to the goodness of such things as nationalism and patriotism. Even though such loyalties can be true virtues, any reader of the Apocalypse – indeed any reader of human history – knows that they have been used in the past as masks for Beasts and their followers.

The Seer also offers us a reminder that Christians seem to need in every age: our commitment to God can bite hard into our own temporal welfare. Many a statement of Christian principle applied to concrete situations has met with the reaction, 'But you have to be realistic!' John was speaking to Christians whose attraction to the Cult Beast and the Great Harlot was based in the realities of their social and commercial life, but the Seer insisted that there was a deeper reality which his hearers had to face. They could only ignore the sinister reality of these figures to their peril. If we give security and success a priority above that of the Kingdom, then we have transferred our worship to Beasts and Harlots, whatever their modern guise.

I will suggest one final point that comes from a very different direction. I know that it was not the concern of John in writing the Apocalypse, but his visions are certainly relevant to it. After the polemics of the Reformation have cooled, it seems nearly laughable that the Catholic Church was identified with the Whore of Babylon and the Pope with the Antichrist (there are some, sadly, who continue to promulgate such identifications even today). But such misapplication challenges the Church to engage in a critique of itself. It would be wrong to make sweeping criticisms of those who instigated practices that belong to a different time and place, but we must examine whether traditions have crept in that today can act as countersigns to the true call of the Church. We must be especially critical of things that seem to come more from the trappings of the Great Harlot than from the God-given adornment of Daughter Zion. Displays of wealth and pomp, courtly honours bestowed upon ecclesiastical dignitaries, elaborate titles and protocols – these things may have validly sprung from human needs and circumstances, but nostalgia and an instinct to preserve

Unmasking the Pretenders (Rev 13:1-17:18)

historical traditions for their own sake hardly provide enough justification for retaining them uncritically today.

The Spirit drew the first century churches along their spiritual adventure by giving them an uncomfortable look at their world. The unmasking would have been painful for many of those who witnessed it through John's eyes. Some undoubtedly tried to deny that the Seer was showing them the true picture at all, yet hindsight shows how accurately John interpreted his times.

Our spiritual adventure depends upon our own willingness to heed the Spirit's voice and to take a hard look at our own world against the truth of the gospel. The Spirit is still trying to draw us out of our naiveté, out of our attraction to what is powerful and successful. The Spirit is also inviting us to break the hold that such attractions have on us, whether as individuals or as churches. The process is not easy. It is not a simple matter to bring anyone, let alone a whole People, down the long exodus road of liberation. Showing us the Beasts that surround us might at least make us more willing to move down the path the Spirit is pointing out to us.

Questions for Reflection and Prayer

1 The Beast from the Sea in Revelation 13 was intended by John to symbolise the Roman Empire, even though no name appears in the text. What sort of force did the Roman Empire represent for Christians in the latter half of the first century in Asia Minor?

2. The Second Beast for John is not presented as a foreign invader, but rather as somehow native to the cities he was addressing, and representing the imperial cult. What connections can be made between the power of the Cult Beast and forces at work in modern societies?

3. The Great Harlot of Revelation 17 is an impressive figure, symbolising Roma – city, empire and goddess all in one – and is introduced by the Seer to contrast vividly with the Woman Clothed with the Sun. Which aspects of the contrast emerge as particularly striking?

4. The Seer aims at unmasking Rome and its empire, despite the resistance his message would receive from some of his hearers.

To what extent can this aim be still valid in today's world, when applied to certain forces. How do you respond to the question, 'Do beasts still lurk?'

8

Some Final Scenes

Revelation 18:1 – 20:15

When the time comes to list the inventions of the twentieth century, there will be many wonderful products to include among its benefits. There will also be a need to analyse whether this or that invention should be seen as a blessing or as a monster.

The slide projector is my personal monster. The fear is irrational. I have actually used this machine with some success, but never with relish. Consequently my experience of the slide projector has been very limited; for all practical purposes it has eventually reduced itself to projecting slides of the Holy Land. My projector-phobia manifests itself in my attitude to the slides themselves. There was a time in which slides from different sources were carefully numbered and kept within their own groupings. In more recent practice, I simply empty the carousel into a plastic bag with the half-hearted resolve to sort them out later. The next slide-show may be a hodgepodge of slides from different visits, slides from other people's visits and commercial slides of varying quality.

The segment of the presentation dealing with the Western Wall[1] would certainly not be six slides in the sequence that they were taken. My plastic bag might yield the following goodies for my audience: (1) a panorama of the Western Wall thronged with pilgrims taken in 1984 – the sunshine was glorious that afternoon; (2) a similar panorama taken in 1983 when the rain was so heavy that the place was deserted – it shows less of the atmosphere, but more of the site; (3) to emphasise the tradition of sacredness attached to the Temple site a close-up of an elderly Jew at prayer by the wall (this one would have to have been purchased); (4) Jack Murphy standing beside a block to show the enormity of the stones that made up the wall; (5) a snap of a modern reconstruction of the Temple complex as it might have looked in the first century; (6) a photo of some of my 1984 group making their own prayer at the wall to point out the chain of devotion that links Jews and Chris-

---

1. Once called the 'Wailing Wall', this impressive masonry originally formed part of the great platform that supported the Temple complex in Jesus' day.

tians. As I fish through my plastic bag, I am not guided by any criterion such as chronological order or keeping amateur photography separate from the ones produced for the tourist trade. Rather, my concern is to gather a few different views of the one location in a meaningful way.

The Seer would have had some sympathy for my approach. Scholars have laboured often and long to discover the intricacies of the Apocalypse's order and structure, but I suspect that much of this toil has been in vain. There is certainly a structure to John's book, but he does not always display a deep concern to order his material according to a wooden logic or some carefully sculpted sequence. John is showing pictures, and some of them are taken from very different angles. Whatever imaginary machine the Seer might have used to weave his work would have to have buttons labelled 'Fast Forward', 'Flashback', 'Freeze', 'Echo' and 'Close Up' – and John would still insist that any two buttons could be pressed at once.

If this book were a commentary on the Apocalypse, John's text would have been divided into sections that are quite different from those that now appear under the chapter headings. Revelation 18, for instance, obviously belongs with Revelation 17 even though I have separated them for our consideration.

Yet there is some justification for looking at Revelation 18 to 20 together, for in this part of the book John is finally showing us the closing scenes from the three and a half years. Like the slides from my plastic bag, these scenes don't all belong to the one collection. We will see things from very different angles, illuminated by very different lights, aligned to very different backgrounds. For instance, John has told us back in 14:8 that Babylon is fallen, yet Babylon is still there to be punished in 16:19. In Revelation 17 Babylon lives at the height of power with any chastisement still in the future. The first part of Revelation 18 contains the announcement that Babylon *has* already fallen, but the end of that chapter announces that Babylon *will* fall.[2] Yes, we might find it confusing. Anyone who imagines that John wanted these visions to fit along

---

2. Compare 18:2 with 18:21. The chronological sequence was not as much of a problem for John as it is for his readers. In the biblical tradition, the prophetic word somewhat collapses hard boundaries between the present and the future: since the word of God's prophet is stamped with divine authority, what the prophet announces has, in a sense, already happened.

a time-line and who tries to reconstruct it is doomed to frustration.

What the Seer has done in presenting the scenes of Babylon's destruction he has also done in gathering all of his scenes of the last days. John has taken various pictures – some snapped in heaven, some on the earth, some through a lens of celebration and others through grief – and constructed a single collage. He wants his audience to experience his multi-dimensional vision of what it means for the 'meantime' to approach its end.

Is it Right to Rejoice?

For many years I have had the privilege of teaching Scripture to future religious educators. As well as lecturing, being a member of staff in a college of education involves sitting quietly in classrooms to observe students practise their future profession. Each supervision clocks up a lot of mileage during these intense periods of teaching practice. Since each school has a distinct character, and since a whole range of humanity is represented by the pupils the student teachers are teaching, this exercise has given me glimpses of what religion means to the school-going population. The attitudes, expressed directly and indirectly in the classroom, spring from different social backgrounds, the influences of home and family, this pupil's level of maturity, that student's recent self-discovery; you would think that there would be very little agreement on such a broad and sensitive topic as religion. Yet there are places where nearly all opinions seem to converge into an eerie near-unanimity.

One such point of convergence that has struck me forcefully is that religion – the Christian religion in particular – is essentially 'nice'. Just as there are times in a French class when any answer to a question is wrong if it is spoken in English, so too young students seem to sense that any response in a religion class will be wrong if it smacks of something negative. In a lesson on being stewards of creation, for example, pupils' responses will reflect a concern for such things as stamping out litter, recycling resources and respecting animals. In a religion class, hypothetical human problems posed by the teacher are discussed and solved with the background presumption that if everyone involved could be caring and reasonable a solution can always be found. The level of care and reasonableness that is presumed would seldom be found in a meeting of a charitable organisation that feeds the homeless. The immediate responses that pupils give in good faith do not necessarily reflect what they expect or do in everyday life, yet the pupils are not being hypocritical, nor do they intend to mislead the teacher or anyone else. They have simply put aside any awareness they may have of the traces of laziness, jealousy, pride and bias that are to be found in any human heart. There is little in the atmosphere of a religion class that hints at the struggles involved in the life of discipleship – struggles that these young disciples meet as soon as the door of the religion classroom is closed and pupils once again emerge into a world tainted with bullying, academic competition, cliques, unprovoked petty malice and other everyday adolescent manifestations of the darker side of being human.

Occasionally children are fortunate to 'grow out of' an affliction like asthma. Unfortunately, many carry the presumption that religion is nice into their adult years. In some people this can be detected by their use of the very term 'Christian' as a simple synonym for being kind; for them, kindness and niceness are so much the essence of Christianity that they have no hesitation in calling a known atheist 'a very Christian person'. The same presumption of niceness can be seen in the sentimental nature of their religion; a quick glance at popular religious art indicates that the association of religion and niceness is widespread indeed.

When such people turn to the Book of Revelation, they encounter a real problem in reading it as the Word of God. The Apocalypse is not a 'nice' book; it doesn't even seem to be aware that it should be. Lest I have given the impression that I think that this confusion between Christianity and niceness only arises with those who are simple and unlearned, I should mention that some biblical scholars have also had similar problems with the book. They find it hard to imagine that some passages in the Apocalypse were composed by an early Christian, or at least by one in good standing. There are parts of Revelation that are so coloured by the negative – violence, vengeance, retribution – that it hard for these scholars to believe that the Good News has penetrated the heart of the author. Sometimes an expert will suggest that parts of the work come from a non-Christian Jewish source, hinting that Jews are expected to meet a far lower standard of niceness than Christians are. Personally I don't really think that such agonising over the niceness of the Apocalypse is in order. And the reason for refusing to agonise over the negative side of the Apocalypse is best expressed by a story.

When I was a young curate, I often carried a pocket New Testament with me. Once I called to the wife of a middle-aged man whose recent heart attack was still a matter of grave concern – we'll call the couple Peg and Michael. Michael had been the manager of a very successful firm in the city and life had been going smoothly. He himself was a man of impeccable character, kindly, conscientious and committed to his faith.

Peg told me the story. Without giving many warning signals, the owners decided to close the establishment that Michael managed. The business was making money, but the owners judged that they would profit more by investing their capital elsewhere. Michael found himself suddenly redundant. With a mortgage and a number of adolescent children, he badly needed the employment that was not likely to come his way given his age and the economic reality of Dublin in the 1970s. The stress had triggered a heart attack and health problems were heaped onto the economic ones.

Peg had many things to worry and be angry about. But Peg's greatest problem that day was the thought that Michael's bosses could make the cold decision to close the firm. She knew these people. They were not monsters. They were kind and decent in many respects. She and Michael had socialised with them on occasion and she had received them into her home. How could they make such a decision so effortlessly and painlessly? Surely they had some inkling of the consequences for families like Peg's? Peg was not just reacting to someone touching her family by their action; she told me of many other employees of that defunct establishment and the problems these people were facing.

We talked for some time. We talked about how businesses make their decisions. We reflected together on how people just have to be given a priority over material things. We bemoaned the hard attitudes that seemed to be taking over human hearts. We wondered if this situation was just a reflection of the way things were going generally, and our common faith in God made us complain that it couldn't be. Then, without really thinking, I reached for my

Testament. Without too much explanation, I read for Peg from Revelation 18, and there was a real consolation in the reading. This kind woman, this gentle woman, this extremely nice person had no difficulty in hearing the voice of God in that text. It gave her hope that the terrible, cold-blooded, murderous system of thought and action that had so damaged her husband's health would be brought to an end. God would see to that; the divine plan could not let something so wounding and mangling rumble along in peace forever.

The Seer projects the fall of the Great Harlot against two very different soundtracks; beginning in Revelation 18, we hear both the rejoicing voices coming from heaven and the choked-up sobs of earthly dirges. But there is something in us that feels more at home with the tone of the earthly dirges than it does with the heavenly Alleluias. The dirges are sympathetic, even though their expressions of pity are rather self-interested. The Alleluias are triumphalistic, judgmental, devoid of compassion. A lifetime of associating Christianity with niceness makes us hesitate in wholeheartedly adding our own Alleluia to those of the heavenly choirs.

At least one commentator has suggested that John himself might have expressed his own small regret over Babylon's destruction – just a superficial regret, mind you, and not enough to produce a real tear. The Seer takes the trouble to list some of the good things that are lost. He possibly didn't feel too badly about the destruction of material wealth, but he lists good things that other parts of Revelation show that he himself values: instrumental music and singing, the warmth of lamplight, the rejoicing of bride and bridegroom. Wasn't there some way to salvage Babylon? The Seer's vision implies that there wasn't.

Peg had no hesitation about which soundtrack best accompanied the vision for her. If Peg had thought that the Great Harlot's destruction was other than visionary – that it was a description of the crushing of real people and everything good within them – she might have paused for a moment or two. But, through a combination of sound instinct and recent experience, Peg knew that the Great Harlot is not flesh and blood; the Great Harlot isn't even a symbol for some grouping of flesh and blood people. John uses the Great Harlot to speak of 'the world' in the worst possible sense of

Some Final Scenes (Rev 18:1–20:15)

the term, not the world created through the love of God but the systems and false worlds that humanity constructs. Through her own experience, Peg recognised that there is a dark system – indeed, a multitude of systems – constructed without God and without regard for divine values, that controls the world we experience and is destructive in its essence. It cannot be tamed and kept safely as a pet that had learned to behave. The wisdom of God that guided the divine act of creation was not the blueprint used for building Babylon. Instead, the Great Harlot was planned on the foundations of power lust, a utilitarian view of human persons, the acquisition of personal and corporate wealth, overriding self-centredness, and the unrestrained search for pleasure. Peg knew that these foundations are very shaky. She wanted to see them rock and to watch Babylon totter with them.

In his condemnation of Babylon, the Seer once more turns the minds of his audience to passages from the prophets, the most important being the condemnation of Daughter Babylon in Isaiah 47. When Isaiah 47 and Revelation 18 are read together, they highlight that Babylon's proud and self-assured attitude has led it to its irrevocable destruction. Daughter Babylon's boasting reflected her blasphemous attitude that nothing could restrain her actions and nothing challenge her supremacy. Peg had to admit Daughter Babylon's might with tears, but Peg will certainly be among those who shout with joy as they welcome Babylon's end.

We have already noted how the Seer echoes the exodus in Revelation 15 and 16 to remind his audience that a liberation of God's People is taking place in these visions. We hear the exodus theme once more in 18:4 as it beckons through the second heavenly voice:

> My people, come out from her! Oh that you may not share in her sins! Oh that you may not receive any part of her plagues!

Ancient Israel had to leave Egypt for their freedom, but certain parts of the exodus story reveal that many left with some reluctance. Along the hard road the Israelites travelled, some longed for Egypt and its fleshpots. They grumbled against Moses. Things hadn't been all *that* bad, had they? Once they lost sight of the evil of their oppression, Egypt still had a nostalgic lure and attraction.

The voice that calls us out of Babylon knows that we are tempted to stay. It has a hard job convincing us that we actually are in an undesirable place. We can appreciate Babylon's comforts and advantages, but we find it harder to acknowledge its dangers.

As we have seen, the Great Harlot was John's way of picturing Roma as the goddess of the imperial cult and as centre of the world's commerce and power. John captured more in this figure than just passing aspects of his contemporary world. The Great Harlot's clothing may come from the world of the Roman Empire, but she fits into fashionable garments from any age. She represents the world of commerce, the systems of power, the human pandering to self and pleasure.

As individuals who benefit materially from the modern world, it is more than our innate gentleness that makes us loath to condemn Babylon outright. We do this by focusing on Babylon's positive side and understating the negative. We might concede that the materialistic world in which we live produces its fair share of casualties, but we will not admit that the system *demands* casualties. We can bemoan the ruination that comes from such things as the abuse of drugs, over-indulgence in alcohol or sexual licence, but we hesitate in linking these to a demand for pleasure that is a basic value in the world around us. We aren't really surprised when we see that the materialist world and the Church come into conflict on specific moral issues, but we fail to see that the conflict goes beyond specific issues, that it reflects a radical difference between the Good News and the vision that the world itself preaches. While Christians do know that they must distance themselves from Babylon at this or that point, they often presume that some peaceful cohabitation is possible. But it's not. The Seer insists that, as long as the Great Harlot survives, she will maim, destroy and murder – and her destructive instincts will be felt most by the People of God. It is of her very nature. There is much that is good in the human world, but its only chance of survival lies in the removal of Babylon.

Voices from Offstage

The casting out of the Dragon from heaven in Revelation 12 allowed rejoicing to break out over heaven's new peaceful state.

Some Final Scenes (Rev 18:1–20:15)

The elimination of the Great Harlot permits a similar heavenly rejoicing on behalf of God's People on earth. The threat is removed, the Great Harlot's deception of humanity has been stopped, and things can now begin to take shape along the lines of the divine plan. Up until now, the Great Harlot has stood in the way.

But we know better than to expect a full and sudden showing of the divine plan. All through the Apocalypse, John keeps tantalising his audience. He keeps bringing us up to a point when we expect to have the climax laid before us in all its splendour, and then he turns our eyes in a different direction. We wait anxiously for the seventh seal to be broken – and all we get is silence. With great expectation, we hear the final trumpet blast, but then a new series of visions begins before the trumpet's echoes have died completely. That penultimate period of three and a half years is mentioned a few times, but what follows it is kept out of our sight. The seventh bowl is poured out and Babylon falls, but the announcement 'It has happened' – just a single word in the Greek – comes as an anticlimax. John isn't playing games with us; at the same time that the Seer is preparing us to understand the finale of the divine plan, he is building up our longing for it to happen. John is trying to make us feel his own impatience at the seeming delay in the process. We, too, must want the ugliness to pass and something glistening with divine beauty to appear.

In 19:5-9 John gives us an assurance that our longing will soon be satisfied, but the assurance comes as John's overhearing of a report from a secret source about a distant happening. The assurance is clear, but wrapped in mystery, its full glory still withheld from us. The Seer does not report this revelation through a direct view of what is going on in heaven, but he hears voices that come from heaven, and these voices know something that John himself cannot know from where he stands. John doesn't even seem to be quite sure whose voices these are; instead he awkwardly tries to describe what they sound like. The message that we get from John's overheard, mysterious offstage voices is that the Bride of the Lamb is ready for the wedding and that the invitations have gone out. But we aren't going to be brought into the celebrations just yet – and we find ourselves being tantalised once more.

However, the message contained in this tantalising scene should satisfy some of our curiosity, for through it John sheds light on a question we were left with from his previous reflections. The Bride is none other than Daughter Zion, and the last we really saw of her was at the end of Revelation 12 when we left her under God's protection in the desert. We were assured of her safety for the time being, but we would hardly have been satisfied had we thought that this scene was the end of her story. John's insistence that this situation was temporary, that it would only last for three and a half years, made us want to know what the end of her story would be. The brief mention of Zion in the vision of the Lamb and his companions reminded us that Daughter Zion was far from being forsaken and alone – even during these three and a half years; but we are now assured that her story is about to be taken up again and that a resolution will come soon. The Bride is ready.

Our appreciation of this fresh image for Daughter Zion might benefit from a bit more reflection on the Seer's use of symbolism – and on how it can be quite different from our own. Our modern use of symbols can be very powerful, evoking instant associations and the strongest of feelings – invading and stirring the deepest parts of our being. One and the same symbol can have quite opposite effects depending on the person who uses the symbol and the audience that receives it.[3] For both the Seer and ourselves symbols can operate in a variety of ways, even contradictory ways.

Although we still use symbols to reach deeply into hidden corners of our being, we differ from the Seer (and other biblical authors) in that we can be more 'intellectual' in our approach to symbols. We have this deceptive feeling that it should be possible to 'explain' a symbol and thus capture most of its meaning. Liturgical symbols, for example, often suffer from such treatment. Many a celebrant thinks that telling the congregation about a particular use of oil in the ancient world is what is most likely to make that symbol meaningful to them; and, of course, such background knowledge can help very much. But such celebrants

3. The swastika serves as a good example of a twentieth century symbol that reaches to both the positive and the negative extremes of association. While in the earlier part of the century, the swastika stood for something that could be paraded and saluted, it is now the grimmest of symbols for that region of the human heart whose existence we would rather deny and for actions that are less than human. There is no single box into which such a symbol can fit, no simple explanation that will capture its significance within a footnote.

can forget that the symbolism really arises from feeling the oil's comforting unction, smelling the rich fragrances which have perfumed it, the warm touch of another human person when the oil is smeared. Consequently, liturgical oils are measured by drops, stingily perfumed and economically applied – and heartfelt questions are asked about the reason for retaining such a meaningless symbol today.

Although we might acknowledge that symbols cannot be exhausted by neat definitions and one-line explanations, we still have certain rules that govern our approach to symbolism. We expect symbols to behave in a logical manner; we speak of the 'mixed metaphor' as an improper use of figurative speech. Not unreasonably, we want a certain modicum of logic and consistency in our symbols and presume we will find it when we investigate the symbolism of a text we are reading. There is nothing wrong with these expectations, but they do not match those of many a biblical author.

Daughter Zion has already appeared as the mother of the Messiah – now she appears as his Bride. Modern readers might well be puzzled by the incongruity of the images. In the real world, the seeming contradiction of roles would make it impossible to think of the Woman of Revelation 12 and the Bride of Revelation 19 as the same figure, but this is not true in John's symbolic narrative. In fact, given the rich lode of biblical texts that the Seer is mining when he speaks of Daughter Zion, this combination of relationships is nearly essential. The Seer is bringing together images for Daughter Zion that were already combined in the biblical tradition. John echoes here the promise of Isaiah 62:5 that Daughter Zion's sons would marry her, that they would add the rejoicing love of Zion as their bride to the devoted love they had for her as her nurtured children.[4] The more logical demands we make upon our symbols would have kept a modern author from complicating the image in this way, but, for the author of Isaiah 62:5 (and for the Seer), the combination of roles does not complicate the picture of Daughter Zion; rather it enriches it.

4. Some modern translations modify the Hebrew text of Isaiah 62:5 to read 'your builder' rather than 'your sons', and there are grounds for thinking that this is what the original author had written. However the text John was using in the first century, whether in Hebrew or Greek, already contained the symbolic clash discussed here.

At the same time that we are told – so very indirectly – of what has happened to Daughter Zion, we are told something more about where things are really heading: the victory celebration will be the wedding banquet of the Lamb and his Bride. Once again, John reminds us that what lies behind the workings of the divine plan is not God's stubborn desire to establish the divine will for its own sake or a divine determination to punish sin. The images and models the Seer presents to us – the great liturgies, exodus, liberation, Daughter Zion, and now the wedding banquet – are ones that emphasise the essential bonds that link God and the Chosen People together. We are never shown divine anger operating out of a concern with abstract offences against objective standards of right and wrong. The wrath of God arises from the unremitting concern God has for the Elect. Similarly, as the scroll of the divine plan is unrolled before us inch by inch, we see that the main image it maps out is a picture of the way the divine love surrounds and directs the Chosen People. We are viewing the divine plan out of focus unless God's love for the Church can be seen clearly at its centre.

At last we are told what the high point of the divine plan will actually be – the marriage of the Lamb and his beloved Bride. Although marriage and the wedding banquet appear in Revelation only towards the end of the book, John is not introducing a new image to his audience. He did not need to build and develop the image himself. It was already a powerful way for communicating such basic realities as the certainty of divine promises, the longings of God's people, their unwavering hope, and hope's fulfilment in a scene overflowing with the joyful and passionate love God has for the Church. John's churches knew the marriage theme already and associated themselves with it deeply.

In Jewish literature, the image of the wedding banquet (ultimately rooted in the prophetic picture of God as the husband of Israel) became a vehicle for conveying the delights of the days when God would fulfil all the promises and hopes treasured by the Chosen People. There was even playful speculation on where the food for such a crowd could be found – Leviathan and Behemoth are the only creatures big enough to satisfy them all, and we are assured that their meat has a wonderful taste. Early Christianity

Some Final Scenes (Rev 18:1–20:15)

developed the image even further: in his parables Jesus likened the Kingdom to wedding banquets and himself to the groom. The New Testament writings speak of the Church as Christ's bride, sometimes using the image to convey the preparations that are being made so that the wedding celebration can take place. The Seer is tapping into an image that spoke to his churches powerfully about Christ, the Church, passionate love and the type of celebration that knows no limits.

Few events are as determined by a culture as the way in which marriage is celebrated. If there is any place in modern urban society where traditions and superstitions can enter undisguised without any embarrassment, it is where weddings are planned and celebrated. Family wedding dresses, something blue, the careful screening of the groom's eyes from his bride ... the list could go on. Couples in twentieth century Tokyo slavishly follow customs that began in ancient Rome and – unbeknown to themselves – a couple in Chicago may be establishing in their celebration today a custom that will affect the weddings of their great-grandchildren. Marriage is the place where the intimate lives of individuals intersect most strongly with the society in which the individuals live, and marriage ceremonies and customs are affected by the interplay.

The two thousand years that have passed since the marriage images were written into the pages of the New Testament have witnessed many changes that affect both our view of marriage itself and the way in which marriages are celebrated. Naturally, our understanding of these images in the New Testament should depend on the marriage customs with which the authors were familiar, even when these differ greatly from our own. It is difficult to reconstruct first century Jewish marriage customs with any great precision, but the attempts to do so provide us with an interesting picture. Unlike our own practice, the first century distinguished between the legal side of marriage and the time when marriage took practical effect. The betrothal was a legal matter, an agreement usually between the families of bride and groom at a time when the couple themselves were little more than children (arranged marriages were the order of the day, remember). After the agreement – which included such details as the size of the dowry the bride would bring with her and the bridal price that the groom's family would pay – the couple were legally husband and wife. Separation between the couple could only be effected by divorce; if the groom should die the bride was considered a widow. But the couple still lived apart for years and they did not have marital intercourse until the second part of the marriage procedures, although it was not forbidden for them to do so.

The second part of the marriage procedures was the wedding. In the mentality of the first century Jewish world, the young girl was considered to be the property of her father until the wedding when she became the property of her husband; in this light, the wedding ceremony could be seen as the groom coming to take possession of his bride. She waited in her old home, surrounded by her family and the women of the community and dressed in all the finery that the community could find. The groom and his friends gathered at his home and eventually moved off to claim the bride. Just as brides are expected to be late today, grooms were often tardy in the first century – delayed by such things as last moments in the company of the men, and the bride's father making a show of demanding a greater bridal price for such a fine young woman. Once the groom finally arrived with his party, a rejoicing procession formed as the bride was brought to her new home and to the banquet that awaited her there, a banquet that seemingly lasted for seven days and seven nights of celebration.

The New Testament reflects images from this picture in its use of the marriage theme. The Church is truly Christ's bride, but the marriage is not yet complete. The Church longs to be brought to the new home that Christ has prepared, and this will happen when he comes again. The time of the groom's coming is not known with precision but, then again, the waiting itself is part of the procedure. Once the waiting is past, there is a fullness of joy and celebration which seven days of earthly feasting can only dimly reflect, and an eternity for the Bride and Bridegroom to be with each other in the consummation of their love. Even now the Church is truly Christ's spouse, but it will take the wedding day to complete the reality of this divine marriage.

As in Revelation 12, our attention is called to Daughter Zion's apparel. She is dressed no longer in her celestial splendour, but in something more splendid still – the shining linen of the virtuous deeds of God's holy ones, her children. This too adds to our understanding of the three and a half year period. It is not simply a period in which Daughter Zion is biding her time; she has spent it preparing herself, and her children have provided her with the wherewithal to do so. Now that the Great Harlot has been stopped in her attempts to usurp the place of the Bride, now that the wedding is announced, the expectation mounts and we grow more impatient than ever for the feasting to begin.

Glimpses of the Victory

Before that happens, however, John tells us of other victories. Many details and important symbols contained in these scenes will not be treated here lest we get lost in them. I will concentrate instead on the unified message that they convey when taken together: these victorious scenes are themselves depicted with an air of something incomplete. Victories though they are, they do not constitute the finale of God's plan.

We are left waiting for the appearance of the Bridegroom – and indeed he appears, but not as Bridegroom. In Revelation 19:11-16, he appears as conqueror of the nations with a name written on his garments that challenges the empty claims of Rome's emperors. His victory is not a bloodletting, for he conquers as the Word of God and his sword is also the Word. The blood on his cloak is his own, his victory a manifestation of the sacrifice he has made as Lamb. This scene of victory is the triumph of God's Word and the defeat of the deceptive lies that governed the nations.

We are left waiting for a banquet, but the one set before our eyes in 19:17-21 is no wedding banquet. We are even told that it is not for us, but for the birds of the sky. There can be a celebration that the Empire Beast and the Cult Beast have met their end, but even that does not warrant God's People entering into unrestrained celebration. They are still expected to wait for something more.

We are left waiting for the appearance of the Kingdom, and a type of kingdom is shown us in 20:1-10. God's Holy Ones can enjoy some triumph here, but Satan still threatens even though he is restrained in some way. The forces of evil will still flex their muscles despite the fact that their attempts are beginning to look very, very feeble. The real Kingdom has not appeared fully, not even yet.

When we put these scenes together, we find that John is presenting us with a very mixed picture of hopes being both fulfilled and unfulfilled. There are good things coming, good things to be enjoyed, even before the divine plan reaches its end. Yet we are to be careful not to confuse the two, not to mistake the small celebrations of victories for the great wedding banquet for which we long, not to imagine that small manifestations of Christ's triumph are the full realisation of the Kingdom, and not to forget about Satan even when he seems to be bound and gagged. The Seer promises us that the road for our spiritual adventure is not entirely rocky, that God has planned some wonderful things for us along its path – but he warns us not to be fully satisfied until we reach its end. He doesn't want us to stop before we reach the goal.

The Seer again draws from Daniel 7 to show us the end of history in Revelation 20:11-15. Like Daniel, John sees the throne that God has set up for judgment. History has provided people with the opportunity to have their names and deeds recorded in the Book of Life, so judgement is the natural conclusion of human history as it reviews all of history's events and evaluates what each person has done over its course. Judgment also brings the great enemies of humanity to an end; Satan, the Beasts, and now even Death and its realm are cast into a pit of oblivion. Everything and everyone that remains is about to be brought into the great finale of God's plan.

John has finally finished with ugliness in his presentation of the visions he has received. As squeamish readers, we might be somewhat relieved by this. Hopefully we haven't made the mistake of thinking that the Seer took some dark pleasure in unveiling these unsavoury realities. He only wanted us to see what is already there and to long for its absence. John's fear is that, by ignoring the ugliness, we will compromise our expectations; we will long for a lessening of the ugliness rather than its complete annihilation. John wants us to settle for nothing less than the full reign of God, to keep marching until the adventure is truly complete. And John assures us that not all is ugliness, that good things await God's People along their path which we are to rejoice in. Still, if we give all of our rejoicing to these things, we have made a mistake. Something even better is to come.

The Church is challenged to be like a first century bride eager for her wedding. Just as we are to be mindful of the threats, we are to look out for the signs that signal the Bridegroom's approach. Good things, such as the triumph of God's Word over the forces of deception, should warm our hearts with the joyful awareness that his approach is not far off. We must also enjoy ourselves as we are being prepared with the fine linen of all the good works that people are doing for the love of God and neighbour. But the joy of the present must be a part of the longing for the finale. We can never settle down in a deception that the most wonderful happening of the present can match the final wonders that are waiting for us in the divine plan. Every blow against Babylon, the Dragon and the Beasts gives us cause to cheer, but we can't match these cheers with the victory songs that we will sing when the Kingdom has its great triumph. Like a first century bride waiting on her wedding day, we are filled with both joy and expectation, but we shouldn't be truly satisfied until the Bridegroom has brought us home.

Questions for Reflection and Prayer

1. What is your response to the popular association of 'religion and niceness', and to the fact that Revelation is not a 'nice' book?

2. The Great Harlot's clothing may come from the world of the Roman Empire, but she fits into fashionable garments from any age. Why is the human psyche loath to condemn 'Babylon', as the Seer would have us do?

3. Daughter Zion becomes the Bride. How can an appreciation of the variety of ways the Seer uses symbols help you appreciate this new image for Daughter Zion?

4. How central to the climax of the Book of Revelation is the image of Bride? Can this image continue to have meaning in our times? How can we as Church today enter into the challenge to be like a first-century bride eager for her wedding?

9
The Grand Finale
Revelation 21:1 – 22:21

Most books and articles that deal with the Apocalypse will point out that the book's very title means an unveiling. As titles go, it is an excellent description of what we have been seeing as we wend our way through its pages. We have seen veils come off various manifestations of the Roman Empire to reveal horrible realities. Other veils have been lifted from the Church, its tribulations and its mission to reveal things of beauty. Most of all, we should feel the veils being lifted from our own eyes. We should be finding that we are looking at things differently. As new lights are made to shine on the objects of our gaze, some things that we once thought precious might now look tacky and cheap. But, more importantly, we might also discover beauty and worth in the places we least expected to look for it.

The process has been gradual. John has tested our patience with the long process of unveiling, especially as he unveiled the ugly and repulsive. Despite the harshness of his imagery and the bluntness of his message, the Seer has actually been very gentle with us. Like someone leading a person from the absolute darkness of a deepest cave into the brightest light of the noonday sun, John has wanted to let our eyes adjust. If he has withheld the glorious reality from us, it was only so that we could really see it without blinding ourselves.

The Road We Have Travelled
When John started us on this spiritual adventure, John's churches saw only the human reality of their local communities with their small joys and woes. The overall plan of God was a thoroughly sealed scroll as far as they were concerned. Reality tended to be defined by the world in which they lived and worked, and the Roman control over that world was, at worst, a fact of life.

William Riley's manuscript ends at this point.

10

It Is Done!

Revelation 21:1 – 22:21

SHÁN Ó CUÍV

If you had not been forewarned in the preface it might have come as a surprise to you, the reader, that Ryles[1] never completed this book. That opening page of chapter nine maintains the book's fluency of thought and expression right up to the last words written. It's just as though he was interrupted in full flight by a caller to his door and would complete the chapter later. In fact the sheer weight of the burgeoning illness halted proceedings on a Thursday afternoon in June, six days before he died.

It was our custom during Ryles' illness that I would read the Scriptures to him and then we would pray the psalms together before he slept. That Friday evening, before we prayed, Ryles made it clear that he could not complete the book. There was no trace of disappointment or failure. His part in it was complete. Now he wanted me to finish it off and have it published if it were worthwhile. I protested my inadequacy for the task, but he pressed me, telling me he would give me some points for the final chapter. He assured me that he did not expect or even wish me to attempt to finish it in his style or as he would have done it.

By the following day Ryles' condition had deteriorated so sharply that he was moved to hospital as a matter of urgency. There he died early the following Wednesday completing his journey in the company of his parents and friends in an atmosphere of prayer and joy. To the end his courage, faith, love, and sense of humour remained intact. Heavily sedated and drifting in and out of consciousness in his last few days, Ryles was still at times acutely aware of what was going on around him. Though very weak he

---

1. William Riley was known by family and many friends and colleagues as Bill. To me and some others he was always Ryles. So much so that he would have been shocked and irritated if he thought that I'd dream of referring to him here in any other way. I ask your indulgence with this usage. It is the only way I can proceed in comfort.

could still express his love and affection for us and draw us into prayer.

He made two mysterious references to the Scriptures in those days. One was an insistence that Isaiah 30 was very important. The other was his repeating of the phrase 'reconciling Jew and Gentile'. He never did, however, manage to give me those promised points and so I am left to puzzle out the ending by following whatever clues I think I have. I cannot claim with confidence that the clues I give are right, still less that my reflections on them tend in the right direction. At most I can only hope that my effort to tackle the puzzle will encourage you to read chapters twenty-one and twenty-two of Revelation and search out its message for the churches and for our lives.

It may seem strange that I have expressed no regret that Ryles failed to complete this book. To me an expression of regret would be somewhat churlish – like being treated to a delicious ice cream on a summer's day and then asking, 'Is that all I'm getting?' It would also be out of tune with the tone of Ryles' life throughout his illness. I can honestly say that those were the happiest days of my life as I was caught up in an unforgettable experience of joy. The only things to be regretted during those days were the shortcomings of our human loving. All else was gift: the faith and hope, the friends, the family, the prayers and messages of support. Even such small details as a visit to the local shop were savoured; even the pain was gift. So often Ryles repeated, 'God will put me through nothing in this world or the next that is not for my good.' There were no 'whys' or 'if onlys' in those months. I will not sully the joy now. No, the incompleteness itself is gift, because it challenges us, the readers, to make our own the quest to hear what the Spirit is saying to the churches.

I said that I have no definite pointers from Ryles but that I have some possible clues. These I will now share. I must bring you back to the Wednesday night a week before he died. Knowing his strength was failing fast he inscribed Bibles he had bought as gifts for his nieces and nephews:

> I leave you the Word of Life. Take it, read it, love it, live it.
> Love always, Your uncle Bill.

This inscription was not composed that night. It was not new. It reflected Ryles' whole attitude to the Word of God. If anyone is to search the message of Revelation 21-22, that must be the basis for it – reading the text over and over, loving the message as the Word of God, and living it as the Word of Life.

But I have another clue from that Wednesday night. In preparation for beginning the last chapter of his book the next day, Ryles asked me to read Revelation 21-22 to him before he slept. I cannot forget the excitement in his voice when he interrupted my reading. 'Read that again – "It is done!" – Give me the Greek Testament... Yes! There it is, one word, *gegonan*, and it appears like that earlier in Revelation, the exact reference I can't recall, but... Ah yes! There it is, almost identical, *gegonen*.'[2]

I'm not sure what the cause of the excitement was. With Ryles I used to wait patiently because I would learn soon enough. But in this case, the final stages of illness closed in so fast that it remains a secret. All I am left with is a memory of excitement and true joy. It's as though 'It is done' was the key, the answer, the fulfilment of a quest. I'm not at all sure what he saw in that phrase but the impression remains of the joy of a dying man that our faith in Christ, that our eschatological hope is much more than wishful thinking. It is in Christ a solid, accomplished fact.

The Bride Appears

In the preceding chapters of Revelation we have witnessed the Lamb's battle on behalf of his beloved people. Now in these last two we get a glimpse of the magnificent final victory. The New Jerusalem appears adorned as a Bride for her Husband. She has been prepared in no less a place than heaven itself. Her preparation has been in capable hands indeed. When the angel carries us to a high mountain we get a glimpse of indescribable splendour. The dimensions and the richness are in superlatives beyond imagining but we are left in no doubt as to the identity of the Bride. The repeated use of twelve – for the tribes of Israel, the apostles, the

2. The phrase 'it is done' [*gegonen*] occurs at Revelation 16:17 in a second perfect singular form. It occurs at Revelation 21:6 [*gegonan*] in a slightly different form, a contracted second perfect plural form: 'they are done' rather than 'it is done' (the plural form at the end of the book might suggest a more comprehensive vision that now '*everything* is completed'.

gates, and in the very measurements of the walls – assures us that the Bride is the Church. Considering the awesomeness of the all-conquering Lamb, his intimacy with the Bride should now be all the more striking. He sets up tent with her and wipes away her tears. Every show of power in crushing evil has been an expression of his love for her. Perhaps the struggles we witnessed with trepidation hid from our eyes the diligent work of the Lamb in preparing his beloved Bride for the wedding.

As John weaves his tapestry of the Bride we cannot but be struck by the variety and brilliance of the Old Testament threads he uses. Those well versed in the Old Testament will have the keenest eye for detail. Still, with even a passing knowledge of Isaiah and Ezekiel, or with the aid of a Bible containing marginal notes that give cross references, we can recognise quotations and allusions to bright promises of restoration and consolation, splendour and intimacy. Now, as John weaves these threads, we see that the Bride is far more splendid than Zion ever hoped to be. The dimensions of Ezekiel's Temple are truly dwarfed by the enormity and perfection of the New Jerusalem. Strikingly, this city has no Temple, since God Almighty and the Lamb are now themselves the Temple. The implication of unimaginable intimacy between God and his Bride, the Church, is obvious. What may not be as apparent is the implication that God's plan is all-embracing.

For John, as we have seen, communal worship is central to our relationship with God. Steeped as he was in Israelite tradition we might expect the Temple to play a vital role in the New Jerusalem. John, however, knew the workings and the layout of the Temple. He knew just how near any rank of Israelite might approach and most of all he knew that Gentiles were totally excluded. By explicitly announcing the absence of Temple in the New Jerusalem John the Seer was proclaiming the removal of any obstacle to Jew and Gentile approaching God together.

Perhaps in his repeating of the phrase 'reconciling Jew and Gentile' in those last days Ryles was drawing my attention to Ephesians 2:11-22 which resonates so well with this theme in Revelation. What Paul sees accomplished in principle in the sacrificial death of Christ, John sees fulfilled in the Lamb's wedded Bride.

It Is Done! (Rev 21:1-22:21) 149

Reconciling Jew and Gentile

Rapid communication, often in the form of searing TV pictures, has exposed us as never before to successive horrors of genocidal conflict in places such as Cambodia, Rwanda and the Balkans, to name but a few. But we would be naive indeed to think that this is anything new. Sadly, no era, no part of the globe has ever been spared the pain of hatred and division. It is an inescapable fact that as far back as the human memory stretches, people are not only alienated from God – they are also alienated from each other. And while there is no denying that ethnic and linguistic differences often lie at the root of these conflicts, one cannot escape the disturbing fact that only too often, as in Ireland, religious differences also play their ugly part. So much so that many people would consider religion an obstacle to peace rather than a means of reconciliation.

Now, in the conflict between Jew and Gentile in the first century AD, John the Seer knew a hostility as intractable as anything we know. And this antagonism had all the explosive ingredients of the ethnic and religious mix. Yet in his vision of the New Jerusalem we see that true religion lies at the heart of reconciliation. In this city the dream of Isaiah 60 is fulfilled, the nations come and walk in the light of God. Perhaps to emphasise the point, John modifies some texts he uses to include the nations in the plan of God. For example, when John alludes to Ezekiel 37:27 ('My dwelling place shall be with them; and I will be their God and they will be my people') in Revelation 21:3, he changes the last word to the plural, 'peoples'. And again, in Revelation 22:2, the healing leaves of the trees of Ezekiel 47:12 are made available for the healing of the nations.

Through thousands of years the people of Israel have managed to combine an acute awareness of their own shortcomings with an indomitable belief in God's love for them, his chosen people. John, with his Jewish background, has brought that gift with him. Though a member of that suspect, suffering, endangered and flawed minority, the early Christian Church, the author of Revelation has not succumbed to the temptation of holding out the hope of salvation for only a beleaguered few. He has instead embraced the divinely inspired vision of salvation extended to countless people of every nation. Since the Fall, Eve's children are helpless exiles, alienated from God and from each other. In chapter twelve John has shown us the Church as Daughter Zion bearing the hopes of all the children of Eve. Now, in chapter twenty-two, at the marriage of the Lamb Eve's exile ends. Access is granted for all the nations to the tree of life (Rev 22:2). Wonderfully, the tree of life is seen to grow within the Holy City. It is within the Church, God's people, that paradise is regained.

The Church at the end of the twentieth century is certainly no beleaguered minority. In fact its very size and influence, and the ease with which so many can belong, could tempt us to lose sight of our grand destiny and dignity as God's chosen people. While scandals, divisions and shortcomings in the Church rightly remind us that we can take no credit for being loved by God, we still need to rediscover the relevance of being Church today. We already see God at work knitting together into one community of faith and hope and love, people of every nation, language and way of life. This challenges us to renew our sense of joy in being Christ's chosen Bride, and to long for the fulfilment in us of his plans for the world.

Choices to Be Made

Ryles' insistence in those last days that Isaiah 30 was very important intrigued me. The chapter contains an oracle against the foolish in the days of Hezekiah who would seek the protection of Egypt in the face of the threat of Assyria. Those who turn to Egypt for protection are condemned for their folly. They carry out no plans of God and so are doomed to failure and disgrace. The Lord himself will deal with Assyria and destroy it and then God's people will rejoice. The people of Zion are urged to trust in God who promises to put an end to their tears. There will be water in abundance to slake the thirst, Jerusalem will be lit by dazzling light and the wounds of the people will be healed. Perhaps most strikingly of all, the people will say 'good riddance' to their idols.

I'll never know if Ryles saw any connection between this and the Book of Revelation, but for me it has highlighted some vital elements in the end of Revelation. Choices must be made. There are real winners and losers. Only those who trust in God will be rewarded.

In the final scenes of Revelation the Beast is slain and the Lamb

It Is Done! (Rev 21:1-22:21) 151

has wed his Bride, but the cowardly faithless and idolaters are excluded from the celebration. Only those whose names are written in the Lamb's book of life may enter. The promise held out is splendid and the invitation urgent. What is on offer to the churches is intimacy with the Lamb and access to the tree of life from which humanity was banished at the Fall.

Each of the letters to the seven churches contains the call: 'Let anyone who has an ear listen to what the Spirit is saying to the churches'. While the contents of the letters vary according to the circumstance, the common element is a call to faithfulness. Only the faithful will be reckoned to have conquered and to them alone is extended the promise of reward. Lest we forget when dazzled by the revelation of reward in chapter twenty-one, we are reminded once again that it is only 'those who conquer will inherit these things' (Rev 21:7).

The reading of the Book of Revelation suggests an image to me. People are gathered in a room to watch a video-recording of some sports event. During the viewing they are called upon to place bets on the outcome. It is a hard-fought contest in which the fortunes ebb and flow, and who it is that has the upper hand is never clear. But the punters have had some assistance. They have been told the outcome of the contest in advance. The question is, can they, or will they, trust the witness, the one who has told them the outcome. The fact of the matter is the witness is the victor and is telling the truth. But only those who placed their bets accordingly will have reason to rejoice when bets are paid.

It takes no great insight to see in life a cosmic struggle between good and evil. It takes no great sensitivity to feel the pain of a world torn with suffering, cruelty and division and which yet longs for peace, love and harmony, It takes no great religious sensibility to be aware of an alienation from God. A pessimist might give the verdict in the contest to the power of evil. An optimist might look in vain to some utopia of human making. But the Christian looks to Christ. In his sacrificial death the Lamb has already conquered. The Beast is slain and the Bride is chosen. The Book of Revelation with all its imagery reveals the final score and urges us to lay our bets. Far from being a book of esoteric predictions of the future, it is a book anchored in the here and now, challenging us to make the right choices. And the choices we make are matters of ultimate life and death.

Come, Lord Jesus!

Ryles sometimes shared with me what he called 'waking thoughts'. These were striking ideas or phrases that sometimes came to him as he surfaced in the morning. On Ash Wednesday 1995, before I brought him to hospital for major surgery, he inscribed for me a card with that day's waking thought: 'All things that come from God lead to God'.

Few people I know could match Ryles' zest for life. The unexpected diagnosis of his illness altered many things, but amazingly caused no lessening of this zest. If anything, his joy and enthusiasm grew. So much so, that the comment was made, 'Ryles taught us how to live and now he is teaching us how to die'. Maybe the keys to living and dying are the same – recognising and welcoming all the blessings of God and letting them lead us to him.

But some of God's gifts are transient, some eternal, and we must distinguish between them and handle them accordingly. If we receive temporal gifts and deny their transient nature we are exposed to a sort of idolatry; miserly, we may be afraid to consume and enjoy them. Then again, we may acknowledge their transience with resentment or regret and, fretful for their passing, become unable to enjoy them. Those who identify God's eternal gifts and embrace them wholeheartedly are the ones who truly know how to live. Confident of the abiding love of God and longing for the fullness of his blessings, they are free to use his transient gifts with generous abandon.

Long exposure to the Book of Revelation had served Ryles well. It had unveiled for him the true nature of many things and had ordered his life with a sound perspective. God now made him faithful to the end. As death approached no panic ensued. He felt no reason to mourn the shrinking of his world and still enjoyed it as it passed. With each successive day his joy increased as he celebrated the imminent fulfilment of God's eternal promises at the wedding of the Lamb. Ryles had always loved that passage at the end of Revelation (22:17):

> The Spirit and the Bride say, 'Come!'
> Let the one who hears say, 'Come!'
> Let the one who is thirsty come.
> Let the one who wishes take the water of life as gift.

Now, fittingly, his whole life took up the joyful cry: 'Amen! Come, Lord Jesus!'

William Riley

(1949 – 1995)

CARMEL McCARTHY, R.S.M.

William Riley was born on 4th September 1949 in Ohio, USA. His primary education took place in Ironton, and he attended St Charles' in Columbus for his secondary education. He came to Ireland in 1969 and entered Clonliffe College later that year, where he pursued studies for priesthood for the Dublin diocese. Early in his student days he became involved in animating a Bible study group in Rathmines, an activity he was to continue on a much broader basis in the years that lay ahead.

Ordained deacon in 1973, his first ministry was in Bayside, where, a year later in June 1974, he was ordained to the priesthood. He continued ministering in Bayside until 1978 and during this period his work with Bible study groups flourished. It was this experience in Bayside and his earlier work in Rathmines that gave rise to his first and one of his most successful books: *The Bible Group, an Owner's Manual*, published in Dublin by Veritas Publications in 1983.

From 1978 to 1980 he undertook postgraduate studies in theology at the Pontifical University of St Thomas in Rome, and obtained a Licentiate in Sacred Theology (*summa cum laude*) in 1980. He was appointed to a curacy in Monkstown parish in 1980 where he served until 1983. Meanwhile, in 1981 he joined the staff of the religious education department in Our Lady of Mercy College of Education, Carysfort, where he lectured in Scripture and in theology until the closure of Carysfort in 1988. During his period in Carysfort he also co-directed a two-year inservice diploma course in religious education for primary teachers, which included a study trip to the Holy Land in 1984.

In September 1983 William Riley left Monkstown, having been appointed to the staff of the Mater Dei Institute of Education as a full-time lecturer in Scripture. Meanwhile, he continued lecturing in Carysfort. Contributing widely to the work of the Mater Dei Institute, he was appointed dean of post-graduate studies, and then registrar, while continuing a full lecturing schedule for undergraduate students.

If his first publication reflected the fruits of his experience in organising and animating Bible study groups, his next two bear witness to his years of teaching. The first of these appeared in 1985 under the title, *The Tale of Two Testaments*. Published by Veritas Publications, and in the USA by Twenty-third Publications, it was attractively illustrated by Theo Payne, with the same high quality of clever line drawings with which Theo had enhanced *The Bible Group, an Owner's Manual*. Twelve months later saw the emergence of yet another teaching tool for Scripture: *The Old Testament Short Story* (co-authored with Carmel McCarthy). Focusing on five Old Testament short stories, this work explored the dynamics of biblical story-telling as a powerful vehicle for communicating spiritual truth and values. Published in the USA by Michael Glazier in 1986, it was warmly received on both sides of the Atlantic.

He spent a sabbatical year at the Pontifical University of St Thomas in Rome in 1986/87 researching a doctoral dissertation which he presented in October 1990, receiving a doctorate in sacred theology (*summa cum laude*) in 1991. This doctoral dissertation was published in a revised form in 1993 in the JSOT Supplement Series (no. 160) under the title, *King and Cultus in Chronicles: Worship and the Reinterpretation of History*.

Dr Riley was a very active member of both the Irish Biblical Association and the National Bible Society of Ireland. He served on the executive committees of both for a number of terms, and was currently vice-president of each organisation at the time of his death. His publications in a number of journals over this period are varied and illustrate the wide range of his scholarly and pastoral interests.

His deep love for the Scriptures as the Word of God was infectious, and former students of Carysfort College, the Mater Dei Institute, All Hallows, and numerous other adult education centres in Ireland, as well as his many friends and colleagues, will remember him for this single-minded zeal that permeated his life as a teacher and scholar. Never satisfied with secondary sources, he loved to wrestle with the Scriptures in their original languages. This was true both for personal prayer and in research. He had a longstanding practice of always making his own translation of any text he was working on. This constant return to the sources coupled with a lively and creative imagination accounted in part for the fresh insights he was continually unearthing. Dr Riley had a rare gift of being able to combine a most rigorous scholarly approach to his research and teaching, with a creative and entertaining facility to communicate the riches of Scripture to audiences of every kind.

Living his love for the Scriptures to the very end, Dr Riley wrote his final book in the last six weeks of his life: *The Spiritual Adventure of the Apocalypse*. This work is a fitting testimony to his creativity and inner resources, and to the values and vision of life imparted to him by his parents, James and Genevieve Riley. Written against the odds of a rapidly advancing terminal cancer with all its attendant pain and unpredictability, the book interweaves into one seamless flow all the different strands of its author's personality. Its pages are alive with a deep personal spiritual vision, made all the more vibrant and urgent by the context in which it was being chiselled. It testifies further to his ability to rephrase and express the essence of Scripture in words and imagery that speak to today's faith issues. The work is undergirded with a rigorous and thorough scholarship that might be taken for granted because of its inobtrusiveness. Finally, this book contains an extraordinary lightness of touch and humour that makes it almost impossible for an unsuspecting reader to guess what it must have cost its author in those last six weeks to have brought this 'Spiritual Adventure' so close to completion.

Dr Riley will be remembered for many qualities: a careful and finely-tuned scholarship, a keen wit and indomitable sense of humour; a deep capacity for friendship; thoughtfulness, sensitivity and integrity, and a lovely disposition to share with great generosity whatever he had – books, music, computer-expertise, as well as those finer gifts of mind and spirit. But at the heart of all these qualities lay one central and all-consuming focus: his passion for the Scriptures as the Word of God. In a world that needed good people he was a strong and kindly light.

William Riley: a Bibliography of Works in Scripture Studies

1981
'Jesus, King and Messiah: a Biblical Consideration', *Scripture in Church* 44 (1981), pp. 486-92.

1982
'Temple Imagery and the Book of Revelation', *Proceedings of the Irish Biblical Association* (hereinafter *PIBA*) 6 (1982), pp. 81-102.

'Wagging the Tale: Biblical Story and Primary Catechesis', *The Irish Catechist* 6 (1982), pp. 6-13.

'Seeing with the Seer', *Scripture in Church* 48 (1982), pp. 526-31.

1983
The Bible Group: an Owner's Manual (Dublin: Veritas Publications, 1983).

1984
'The Gospel of Mark: Why the Community Should Reclaim Its Property', *Scripture in Church* 56 (1984), pp. 466-70.

1985
The Tale of Two Testaments (Dublin / Mystic CT: Veritas Publications / Twenty-Third Publications, 1985).

'Situating Biblical Narrative: Poetics and the Transmission of Community Values', *PIBA* 9 (1985), pp. 38-52.

1986
(With Carmel McCarthy) *The Old Testament Short Story: Explorations into Narrative Spirituality* (MBS, 7; Wilmington, DE: Michael Glazier, 1986).

'Changing Fortunes: Wealth and Poverty in Luke's Gospel', *Scripture in Church* 62 (1986), pp. 228-32.

1988
'The Book of Job and the Terrible Truth about God', *Scripture in Church* 71 (1988), pp. 322-26.

1990
'On the Location of Meaning in a Sacred Text', *PIBA* 13 (1990), pp. 7-23.

'Perceiving the Cosmos: Wisdom Literature as a Source of Creation Theology', *PIBA* 13 (1990), pp. 42-57.

1993
'The Shapeless God of Israel: An exploration of the aniconic tradition of biblical religion', in D. Lane (ed.), *Religion and Culture in Dialogue, a Challenge for the Next Millennium* (Dublin: The Columba Press, 1993), pp. 40-63.

'Looking beyond Death in the Hebrew Bible', in D. Harrington (ed.), *Death and New Life: Pastoral and Theological Reflections* (Dublin: Dominican Publications, 1993), pp. 83-89.

King and Cultus in Chronicles: Worship and the Reinterpretation of History (JSOTSup, 160; Sheffield: JSOT Press, 1993).

1995
'Who is the Woman in Revelation 12?', *PIBA* 18 (1995), pp. 15-39.

1997
The Spiritual Adventure of the Apocalypse (Dublin / Mystic CT: Dominican Publications / Twenty-Third Publications, 1997).

Contributors

Carmel McCarthy RSM lectures in Hebrew and Syriac in the Department of Near Eastern Languages, University College Dublin, and co-authored *The Old Testament Short Story* with William Riley (Wilmington DE, 1986). She is also the author of *The Tiqqune Sopherim and Other Theological Corrections in the Masoretic Text of the Old Testament* (Fribourg and Göttingen, 1981), *St Ephrem's Commentary on Tatian's* Diatessaron: *an English Translation of Chester Beatty Syriac MS 709 with Introduction and Notes* (Oxford, 1993) as well as numerous articles in books and scholarly journals.

Shán Ó Cuív, a priest of the Dublin diocese, is moderator of the Cherry Orchard parish, Dublin 10. Through close association with William Riley over the years since 1970 he would describe himself as 'an apprentice' in the Scriptures, and indebted to his friend for numerous rich and invaluable insights. In addition to his many parish commitments, he has derived particular satisfaction from animating and facilitating Bible study groups in the various parishes in which he has served.